How We Found Our PRIDE

LETTERS TO A YOUNG QUEER

produced by
FLOYD STOKES

edited by
M. DIANE McCORMICK

introduction by
RON CLAIBORNE

A publication of the American Literacy Corporation

Produced by Floyd Stokes.
Graphic Design by Sheena Hisiro.
First Edition, 2021. All rights reserved.

ISBN 978-0-9960857-6-2

PRINTED IN USA

Dedicated to the writers whose letters bring these pages to life. Thank you for sharing your stories to help others heal. May your voices ring on.

A note from the editor: Times change, and language changes with them. The beauty in this project is that our writers come from many generations and cultures. We love the unique voices they offered. We chose to keep their varied references to the LGBTQ+ community – which is, of course, on a wondrous journey of its own.

CONTRIBUTORS

CHAPTER 6

CHAPTER 7

CHAPTER 8

CHAPTER 9

CHAPTER 10

AFTERWORD

FROM PRIDE COMES STRENGTH
An Introduction by Ron Claiborne

When I read the letters in this powerful volume, I saw themes that many of them shared even as they recounted their unique stories. In account after account, the writers describe their confusion, resistance, uncertainty, fear – but ultimately their acceptance and joy in coming to terms with their truth and finding a welcome in the LGBTQ+ community.

These stories are moving and inspiring in their candor, honesty, and meaning for not just queer people but all people. All of us, LGBQ+ or straight, ultimately are forced to confront enduring questions of identity: Who am I? Who I am really?

For generations, the binary world, much like the dominant white culture of America, has taught us that to be different is to be a lesser human being, an outsider, a freak. Someone once branded with terrible slurs about their gender identity was even considered deviant or, quite literally, a criminal.

What a terrible construct to have to fight against and overcome! The stories in this book remind us that this battle can be fought and won. On the other side of that often painful struggle is liberation.

My LGBTQ+ friends have told me stories of being painfully closeted, parents who rejected them, and struggles to be accepted as people. Every one of them also tells of a kind of rebirth and exhilaration once they shook free of the shackles of oppression.

When I was a reporter at ABC News in the Boston bureau, I covered the landmark legal battle in Massachusetts that led to the legalization of same-sex marriage. In truth, I did not at first understand why it was so important that gay couples be allowed to marry. Why not accept the compromise that Vermont had authorized: Civil union?

I interviewed one of the couples suing for the right to marry. When I asked one of the women why she and her partner wanted to wed, she said her daughter, maybe 9 years old, had said to them: "If you love each other, why don't you get married?" The answer, of course, was that they couldn't because same-sex couples were prohibited from marrying.

Like a revelation, I suddenly, belatedly understood that gay, lesbian, and so many other Americans on the gender spectrum were victims of a profound wrong, not just because they could not marry but because they, as we Black Americans, had been victims of a terrible injustice. The letters in this book rarely acknowledge that injustice in explicit terms, but if you read carefully, you'll find the recurring subtext.

Within these stories – gritty and witty, painful and hopeful, cautious and honest – you may notice that the writers omit one thing that stood out to me. They don't mention their strength. That's not just due to their humility, I believe. It's also because they don't have the distance from their own narratives to see what we, their readers, can see: That it took tremendous strength to confront, resist, and overcome the forces arrayed against them telling them what and who they should be in order to discover and embrace who they really are. For that and more, they have earned the pride that they celebrate and that we celebrate with them.

Ron Claiborne

Ron Claiborne is a retired journalist and ABC News correspondent.

CHAPTER 1

"I think being gay is a blessing, and it's something I am thankful for every single day."

- Anderson Cooper

CHAPTER 1

NOTES

"What are you?"

Dearest You,

I don't have a magical "Coming Out" story to share, mostly because I have never felt the need to explain myself to anyone. But just because no one ever pushed back against me doesn't mean that I choose the easy path. Life is a constant process of growth, reinvention, resisting labels, and challenging yourself to be your best person at every turn.

Growing up in Virginia Beach, I was given the freedom to be whoever and whatever I chose. My parents were military parents and shockingly laissez-faire about the details as long as I was getting good grades and staying out of trouble. They let me make my own decisions and deal with the outcome in stride, and I was always free to express myself in whatever medium I chose. I always had just assumed that the way that I felt and walked in the world was the default setting.

It was not until I went to a friend's bachelorette party – a lesbian friend's bachelorette party, filled with people up and down the LGBTQ+ spectrum – that I realized that I was attracted to people who weren't male. I was confronted with a frank question about my sexuality: "What are you?" I didn't have an answer. That's how I came to be 26 and just realizing that I was queer.

It is an interesting feeling to see yourself through a drastically new lens, to learn that who you always were doesn't have to be who you always are. There is a comfort and freeness that comes with realizing that there are still pieces to the puzzle missing.

It took some time, but in discovering my queerness, I put some more of my puzzle together. And yet, I know that there will still be more to come. I also realized that to be queer doesn't mean you have to define yourself by a label. Labels are stagnant, and your sexuality and identity can evolve over the course of your life. Your presence in this world is a gift. In the course of your life, there will be several moments where you reinvent what it means to be authentically you. Each time, you will bring something new and beautiful to the table. Embrace where you are in your journey, and take nothing for granted.

Enjoy the process of learning about yourself. Spend time each day asking yourself who you are, what you stand for, and what you want out of this life. Try out different things until you find things that fit! You get to make your own path. You don't have to conform to any other prescribed way forward. Think outside the box and reach for the stars, my friend. At the end of the day, know that YOU are your own wildest dreams come true.

All my love,
Tina

Tina Zeigler is a queer public-school teacher who grew up in Virginia Beach, Virginia. She is an outspoken advocate for LGBTQ+ youth, access to mental wellness care, and racial justice. She earned her master's degree in teaching from Shippensburg University. Tina teaches chemistry at a high school in Carlisle, Pennsylvania, and she enjoys spending time with her spouse and two dogs.

"It turns out, they were right."

Dear Friend,

Fear is a powerful thing, but in my life, I have learned that you can't let fear hold you back from being who you are.

I grew up in a Catholic family. My father and his family were very athletic, but I preferred playing with girls instead of playing football and baseball. From the time I was in kindergarten, I'd see a couple and be attracted to the male. I didn't know the word "gay," but I knew my feelings just weren't "normal."

When I was 12, two of my older cousins, who lived next door and were like sisters to me, came out as gay. One cousin's children were taken away from her because she was a lesbian. Sadly, nobody in my neighborhood felt sorry for what my cousins were going through. Instead, everyone said my cousins were "weird." They were "bad."

I knew I had feelings like theirs, but I swore that I would never act on them because I wasn't willing to give up my family or be looked at like a second-class citizen. I got married to a woman I met in college. I adopted her son, and together, we had two more children.

Unfortunately, our outlooks on life differed, so we agreed to separate. I missed my kids so much, but the marriage was over.

And then it happened. My friends were all saying I would get married again, but I didn't want that - not in the way they meant. That's when I said to myself, "I've never accepted myself for being gay."

I was in therapy and told my counselor that I was probably gay, and he became very uncomfortable. So I dumped that counselor and found another - a former Mennonite woman who helped me understand myself and accept myself. She even helped me come out, even though I worried about things like losing my kids, and how my parents would react.

I had read a lot of books saying that once you come out, things get better. It turns out, they were right. My mother just wanted me to be happy. My kids moved in with me. My career didn't suffer. I built stronger relationships with my family because I was honest with myself.

Today, I have a healthy, 20-year relationship with my now-husband, Chris. I feel like I've come so far, and I really do believe that you have to be true to yourself. Maybe I wish I could have accepted myself sooner, but I love that I'm a father and a grandfather.

Fortunately, your generation doesn't have to choose between being yourself and parenthood. If it's important to you to have kids, then you can. The important thing is that you be honest with yourself, no matter what. You have nothing to be ashamed of. Whether you're religious or not, I believe that God made all of us, and God does not make mistakes.

If your family doesn't accept you, that's not your fault. That's the family's problem. Build a circle of friends you can depend on, because family doesn't always have to be related by blood.

And don't be afraid to seek help. There is no stigma to asking for help, whether from a professional therapist or a trusted friend.

It's so true. Life really does get better. When I was 14 years old and trying to figure out how to not be gay, I could never have imagined that I would have the happiness in my life that I have today. Stay true to yourself. That makes all the difference.

All my love,
Dave

Dave Skerpon, SVP, Enterprise Marketing for Capital BlueCross, leads a talented team of marketing professionals. He joined Capital BlueCross in 2007 after 23 years in banking. He is a committed community volunteer, having led successful annual campaigns for the United Way of the Capital Region, Cultural Enrichment Fund, and Allied Arts Fund. David and his husband, Chris Baldrige, live in Harrisburg, Pennsylvania. David is a father of three and grandfather of two wonderful grandchildren.

"I call out injustice when I see it."

Dear Friend,

If you're looking for unicorns and rainbows, turn the page. But if you want a real-life story about growing up the hard way and still finding that strong person inside, keep reading.

I was raised with my grandmother. The family was Christian Baptist. I wasn't exposed to the LGBTQ community. I finally asked a close friend: Is it normal to have feelings toward the same sex?

"Oh, sure," she said. "Happens all the time."

So there I was, thinking this must be normal, but knowing somehow that my family would call it an abomination. I got mixed up in a situation at school – a girlfriend was interested in another female, and it came back to me, and things just went downhill from there. I called my aunt. She kind of knew. We talked for an hour. I didn't want to scare my grandmother – not about her learning that I was gay, but that I would be expelled.

My grandmother did learn I was gay, and she wasn't the happiest about it. But some things just can't last. It came to a point where I didn't stop my lifestyle. Then one day, my grandmother's own mother died, and I had rarely seen her so emotional. It opened a crack, and we finally talked – really talked. This is who I am, I told her. I'm not living anyone else's dream. I'm living mine.

Seeing who I really was finally changed her. Now, she's very accepting. Whoever I'm with, she'll address. She'll buy them gifts. She'll include them in family dinners. Give people time to grow, I know now, and see things through their eyes, and you'll find that you're growing with them.

Let's back up, though. I went through a lot as a teenager. Being LGBTQ was "accepted" but still looked down on. I self-medicated. I used recreational drugs. Things finally changed when I saw the dark place I was in.

I'm outspoken. I call out injustice when I see it. Even in Black Lives Matter, they were separating LGBTQ Blacks from the protests. I was like, "Why? We're all Blacks, fighting for Black lives."

I'm big on spending time with kids, talking about health and wellness. I don't care if I have to sit and play Fortnite for two weeks with a 14-year-old if it means giving them a safe haven and a space to finally express how they feel.

You have to get around people you can understand and who understand you. Reach out for community resources. Find them by searching online and talking to friends and trusted advisers.

Value your body, and make others value and appreciate you. Plus, don't let your feelings stack up on the shelf. Deal with them head-on. Get therapy. There's no shame in that. And find ways to vent through art, writing, music.

I can honestly say that I'm in a very comfortable place in my life. I have a health condition called lupus and thought I could never have children, which was terrible to me, but I found a fertility clinic and now I have a 3-year-old daughter – and that's not all. I'm also raising two teenage nephews. My life is very full.

As for my grandmother, look at her journey. She was born in a small town in Alabama. It took some time, but she's the same person who's now saying, "If you want me to attend your wedding, I sure will. I'll walk you down the aisle."

Prejudice and hate can be killed. We can battle this together. Real love will conquer it all.

With hope and confidence,
Tamika Wesley

Tamika Wesley was born in Eutaw, Alabama, but raised in Harrisburg, Pennsylvania, by her grandmother. She has worked in the mental health field and wanted to do more for her community, so during the pandemic, she established a commercial cleaning company and a non-profit organization to give back. "To say I am blessed would be an understatement," she says, "and I am just thankful for my growth as an individual."

"Suddenly, I heard a voice."

Dear Friend,

My story is about accepting myself while seeing my journey through the eyes of my loved ones. It's about the love that kept me from committing suicide. It's about earning respect and helping others find their paths.

At 6 years old, I'd never heard the word "transgender," but I knew I was different. I played with my sister's dolls. I'd rather hang out with my girl cousins than the boys. As a teenager, I would wear my mom's clothes when my parents went away.

When I was 10, my dad insisted that I make some guy friends and do guy things. I found two guys who are still my best friends today. They taught me to fish and hunt, and guess what? I didn't like it, and that was a good thing. It helped me decide who I really was.

Still, I had a long way to go. I married a woman. Two months later, I told her about my identity, and she gave me the freedom to be who I was – but only at certain times. We had a daughter.

Over time, my wife became more accepting, but there were a lot of fights. One day, she asked me to see things through her eyes. How would I like it if she were transitioning? Not much, I realized. I didn't marry a guy, and she didn't marry a female. As I saw things from her perspective, she gave me more room to be myself and go out as a woman.

Then one night, we had a big fight, and I thought I couldn't take it anymore. I rode my four-wheeler to a mountaintop where I like to think. I pulled out a pistol and put it to my head. Suddenly, I heard a voice. My mother had died a year before, but it was her voice, saying, "No, don't do it!"

That stopped me. When I told my wife what happened, she said that I was ready for the transition to a woman. I hesitated, but she insisted. I spent three years on hormone replacement therapy and then had surgery. Since then, our marriage has never been better. I think we'll be retiring together on the beach.

As you can see, we learned to make communications a priority. With communications, you build honesty, trust, and respect. Family and friends are more apt to accept who you are and support you. And in reality, nobody has to accept you, but you can darn sure ask for that respect.

I've also found that giving back is so important. As I transitioned, I vowed to get out in the community, be noticed, and make people aware that we are here. People find that to be very helpful. I have advocated for the homeless and for trans kids. I was the first openly transgender woman for run for Pennsylvania state office. I even helped an Amishman transition and gain the acceptance she needed to stay with her church and her family.

Years ago, I avoided public speaking. The thought terrified me. After my transition, I realized that what I hated was putting my true self in front of people. Now, I speak all the time, sharing my story and advocating for others. I can live now as I do - being myself, speaking my mind, enjoying time with family and friends – because I am who I am. I don't have to hide.

Neither do you.

All my love,
Janelle

Janelle Kayla Crossley, of Newville, Pennsylvania, honestly believes in equity, equality, and justice for all. Now in semi-retirement, she works for Community Cares, a nonprofit providing resources and shelter for the homeless. Her community advocacy for gender identity includes advising court systems on addressing issues involving children on the gender spectrum. In 2020, she ran for state Senate and made history as the first openly transgender woman to run for state office in Pennsylvania.

"She knows that God has given her some great gifts."

Dear Friend,

I could write as an ally and a public official dedicated to LGBTQ rights, but most importantly, I am a parent of a proud, outspoken gay daughter who has taught me so much about finding your identity and standing up for your beliefs.

My daughter, Alexis, was around 14 when she made it known that she identified as gay. She didn't always have an easy time. She struggled with issues of personal identity, which is an issue that everyone wrestles with in life, regardless of gender or sexual orientation. My father, Lex's own grandfather, clung to rigid ideas from his generation about the things supposedly "wrong" with LGBTQ people.

All I ever wanted was to be the best support person possible for my daughter, no matter what phase of life she found herself in. And in time, I saw with my own eyes that love really does conquer all. My father's love for our Lex overpowered his outdated values. Regardless of her sexual identity, he chose to support her.

At the end of the day, the people that we truly love and are truly a part of us need to know that we've got their back, no matter what. Ultimately, it's our role to support the best person that God intends them to be.

I've learned how important it is to have advocates for the LGBTQ community in our lives. I'm an elected official, and Lex reminds me constantly of the positions I should be taking that protect the rights of everyone I represent.

She is a constant reminder that government can never write a one-size-fits-all solution to the problems out there. There should be – and are – services and help available for those who are struggling with their identity, or who face discrimination because they identify as LGBTQ. My job is making sure that our laws and government services are sensitive and culturally competent to the challenges that each individual is facing, regardless of their circumstances.

Everyone should be an ally. Just because issues in the LGBTQ community don't affect you directly doesn't mean you don't have a responsibility in advancing solutions. Equity and inclusion should be for everyone, especially members of the LGBTQ community.

My daughter is an amazing young woman with nerves of steel. No matter the issue, she stands up for what's right, with arguments that are well thought-out and not based on stereotypes or disinformation. She doesn't look to anybody for approval. She knows, deep down inside, that God has given her some great gifts, and she's never, ever afraid to use them.

She has charted out her course to her dream of owning her own construction business someday. I have no doubt that she will get there. She has my unconditional love.

As you read this letter, I hope you know that you, too, have allies. Maybe they're not obvious to you, but they exist. If you're struggling, help is out there, starting with your local government human services agencies devoted to helping people find the right path in life. Reach out for help from your community or from the people around you, and they will become your support network. I promise – they will help you find the way.

With admiration and support,
George Hartwick

George Hartwick is a proud native of the diverse, tight-knit, blue-collar town of Steelton, Pennsylvania. His own obstacles in life include degenerative disease that put him in leg braces as a child but didn't stop him from becoming a champion wrestler. As a longtime county commissioner for Dauphin County, Pennsylvania, he has used his office to help people find jobs and homes, celebrate their diversity, shed addiction and crime, and pursue their dreams.

CHAPTER 2

"If you help elect more gay people, that gives a green light to all who feel disenfranchised a green light to move forward."

– Harvey Milk

CHAPTER 2

NOTES

....

....

....

....

....

....

....

....

....

....

....

....

....

....

....

....

....

"Were we mocked and jeered? Not at all!"

Dear Friend,

Thank you for picking up this book and reading these testimonies. As you read about my personal journey, I hope you come to know that you are not alone. You can accept yourself for who you are while you come out to yourself, your friends, family and co-workers. Please know that growing into your feelings and reactions is normal. This life is yours. Find the emotional power to walk the path that is yours alone.

Maybe you belong to a religious family where identifying as LGBTQ+ is frowned upon? I grew up in such a family. I grew up in a devout Roman Catholic family and attended Roman Catholic schools through graduate school. I was always taught that homosexuality was wrong, evil and a "mortal sin."

When I was in the sixth grade, I began to realize I was different, sexually. I had crushes on some of my male friends and was attracted to a few male models I had seen in magazines. I even was attracted to some of my male teachers, who were mostly priests. I was not interested in girls or in the straight-orientation pornography often shared by friends.

I never expressed those thoughts or feelings to anyone. I feared that someone would find out, and I would be mocked, beaten or belittled. At times, because I knew of no LGBTQ+ people in my family or mostly Polish-ethnic, Roman Catholic neighborhood, I felt lonely and thought there was something wrong with me. I remember relatives once referring to someone they knew as "light in his loafers." I knew this had nothing to do with shoes.

Impressed by the "religious individuals" who educated me, I wanted to be a teacher, and I thought the only way to do that was by becoming a priest myself. That was when I encountered a welcome surprise. Here I am, a teenager entering a Roman Catholic seminary, and I discovered that I could talk about my sexual preferences and act on my feelings with classmates and teachers who were closeted themselves. We were forced to stay closeted for fear of being thrown out of the seminary and thus embarrassing our families and friends.

My time in the seminary opened a new awareness in me. I started realizing I was not alone and not unusual, even though my religion continued to tell me that being a homosexual was a sin and that I would end up in hell. It was only when I left the seminary, with a gay classmate, that I was able to begin accepting a truer and freeing identity.

That classmate became my partner and is now my husband. We lived a closeted life for our first 20 years together, fearing physical harm and job loss. Finally, on the day of my inauguration as president of HACC, Central Pennsylvania's Community College, I publicly announced my sexual orientation by thanking my husband for his support of 30 years.

Were we mocked and jeered? Not at all! In fact, my husband received more applause than I did!

Even though being LGBTQ+ continues to be normalized in today's society, the journey to self-acceptance takes many routes and is an ongoing process. Be gentle and patient with yourself, especially when people disown you or show disdain. Know there is a strong support system ready to care for you. Always remind yourself that your mental, emotional and, yes, spiritual well-being depends on your ability to know and love yourself. You must! When you do, you will be able to achieve genuine relationships with others.

Onward you go, proudly!
Love,
John "Ski" Sygielski

John J. "Ski" Sygielski, Ed.D, has been president of HACC, Central Pennsylvania's Community College since July 2011. He serves on boards for community college associations, economic development, and Harrisburg's Recycle Bicycle. Ski and his husband, Steve Perrault, live in Harrisburg, Pennsylvania. A native of Cleveland, Ohio, he is an avid bicyclist and the only member of his working-class family to graduate from college.

"He said, 'Yeah. No duh.'"

Dear Friend,

It was Christmas Eve. I was in the middle of a divorce from a hetero marriage. I had cut my hair short. Someone told my mom they thought I might be gay.

So my mom asked me, "Are you bisexual?"

How are you supposed to answer when the time just isn't right? I simply wasn't ready, so I kind of blew it off. The truth would emerge in time, but I learned a valuable lesson that day. Take the path to acceptance and disclosure on your timeline. Don't let others force it on you.

I grew up in a large Irish-Catholic family. My mom had a difficult childhood, and I am grateful that she had a safe haven in the church. But it was a world of rules and expectations. Sex was for marriage, between a man and wife.

My first kiss was with a girl, in second grade, but I dated boys. In college, I was absolutely gaga over some of the girls, but I convinced myself that feeling fireworks going off inside was the way friendship worked. Then I made out with a girl, and I finally realized this could be part of who I am.

Even while I wondered what that meant, I married a guy. Honestly, even he knew I was attracted to girls. We got divorced a couple of years ago, and that was when I recalibrated. Why was I trying to live my life the way that everyone else expected? Now it was time to try it my way.

The two years since have been transformative. I came out to my friends first. When I came out to my brother, he said, "Yeah. No duh." He wasn't the only one. What a surprise to me! The people who truly love you, I realized, want you to be comfortable with coming out on your own terms.

Even my parents responded better than I anticipated. I had been so busy writing the narrative for them that I almost, in my mind, blocked them from drawing their own conclusions. I was petrified by some sort of phantom that turned out not to be real. They are my parents, and they want me to be happy, safe, and loved.

Yes, there have been challenges. I've noticed that people trying to "understand" the LGBTQ community think in terms of sex instead of relationships, and that can lead to some wildly inappropriate questions. In those cases, one valuable way to set boundaries is to say, "I don't know. Google it."

Remember that bisexuality is a valid sexuality. You can find attraction, not in gender, but in chemistry and in the spark in a person's eyes when they talk about the things they're passionate about.

Anyone who tries to invalidate your sexuality is not your person, and that's okay. Surround yourself with queer friends. I discovered the joys of the drag community, where there's so much caring and passion. I also found a gym with a lot of LGBTQ members. Even if we identify differently, we find compassion and understanding in our shared stories.

My life today is so much better than the 14-year-old version of myself. I feel authentic. I feel connected to other humans in ways that wouldn't happen if I were closeted. I feel true joy. It's not an incomplete joy when I accomplish something or when I'm in love. I live my life fully, and I get to share my complete, authentic self with the people I love. You can do the same.

All my love,
Shelby

Shelby is a queer woman living in Richmond, Virginia, with her cats Opie and Loki. Her favorite days are spent with her Dad, Mom, Brother, and his girlfriend spending time together making memories. She counts herself blessed for her incredible, fun, large family and is thankful for her extended family she has built through her friends and community. Shelby loves to explore National Parks and has a goal to visit them all.

"In my classroom, I teach love."

Dear Friend,

I grew up in a Christian family with conservative beliefs. From an early age I was taught that being gay was a sin. Fortunately, I can tell you that people grow, change, and accept. It's here in my story.

I have profound memories of family and friends expressing disdain and disgust towards queer people and queer relationships. Those memories stick with me, even when I know that people have evolved in their beliefs.

In seventh grade, I knew that I was gay. I knew that I was different. I looked at boys more than girls, but I made myself believe that I admired them and just wanted to be friends. Deep in my heart, though, I knew what I wasn't ready to accept. I told myself I never would accept it.

I attended college in New York City where I stepped one toe out of the closet, and with fear, jumped right back in. I thought I could further closet myself by transferring to a tiny conservative Christian college in Western Pennsylvania. With the exception of a few short moments, I stayed fully closeted.

It wasn't until I was 22 years old that I fully came out. It was FAST. I had started taking anxiety medicine – which I realize now I needed because I was insisting to myself that I could never be who I truly was. Ironically, taking that medication allowed me to breathe, and I came out to my family, friends, and publicly within only two months.

My coming out experience was better than I expected, and I feel incredibly privileged for that. Here I am at 26 years old. My immediate family and most of my extended family have a great relationship with me and my boyfriend. I, as well as members of my family, have done a lot of growing. We have questioned and challenged the belief systems that led us to why we believed what we did.

Now, I am a second-grade teacher. My greatest desire for my students is that they be relentlessly who they are. Children need to feel free to express who they are and who they want to be without hesitation. In my classroom, I teach love, acceptance, and an appreciation for all things different from you.

Differences make our world unique. Through the power of books, I can expose my students to so many different topics. They can see through literature that not everyone has one mom and one dad. Not everyone has parents of the same skin color. Not everyone is even raised by a parent.

There is no bigger heart and no heart more understanding than that of a child. Hate is taught. Disdain towards differences is taught. Seeing the love my students have for everyone, love that is without boundaries and without limitations or expectation, gives me hope. I long for my students to see their teacher, who is queer, being relentlessly himself.

Twenty or 50 years from now, I want each of my students to look back and be able to say that I loved them and accepted them for exactly who they were, as a perfect human being. I want them to leave second grade knowing they are worthy of love just as they are. It's the same thing I wish for you.

All my love,
Derek

Derek Witmer is a second-grade teacher from Harrisburg, Pennsylvania. He is in his fourth year of teaching and is K-2 Social Studies Department chair, co-lead of his school's STEAM team, and serves on the Social Emotional Learning Committee and the district's Equity and Inclusion Committee. He is passionate about meaningful technology integration and inclusion of diverse literature. He loves being outdoors and spending time with his dog, Cooper, his boyfriend, and his family. "Simply put," he says, "I love where I am in my personal and professional life."

"My friends noticed that my confidence was skyrocketing."

Hey,

Quick fact about me: I don't like not knowing things. Or, even more frustrating, knowing that I don't know or understand something. Especially things about myself.

I grew up in a church with a social justice mission, but conservative beliefs. Attending public school broadened my horizons, but still, I didn't understand gender identities other than male and female. (I knew transgender people existed, but it was theoretical. I didn't know anyone who was trans.)

As for me? I didn't exactly fit those categories. The things I didn't "like" were my brain's way of telling me I was different. I didn't "like" having long hair, so I didn't take care of it, leading to all kinds of tangles and issues. Showering was unpleasant, to say the least, because I had to face a body that didn't match what I felt it should be. (Pro tip: you CAN shower by nightlight. Just be safe.)

And clothes! Skirts? Dresses? Ew! I didn't just dislike them - they felt WRONG. And bras? Ugh. Not because they were uncomfortable – I mean, that's the way bras are – but because they emphasized what I wanted to ignore.

My sister and I would joke about my affinity for shopping in the men's department. Funny enough, even though it wasn't my first moment of gender euphoria, an important one was when I got my first boxer shorts via a friend of hers. (Long story.)

Obviously, there's more to gender than dresses and bras and boxer shorts – oh, my! – but these moments add up. I was in my 30s when I learned that gender isn't either/or. First, I identified as agender, and then genderqueer. I've landed on transmasc nonbinary (and I still hang onto genderqueer.) Labels are funny things. They can be limiting when others put them on us, but, dang! Finding your own label(s) can be the most freeing thing in the world!

Another part of the journey to finding my authentic self was changing my name. The world knew me by a name that was after my grandmom (who I loved, and love, dearly).

As much as I loved that my mom chose to name me after her mom, and even though I carried their last name, they just didn't fit anymore. So, on June 1, 2019, I announced my "rebranding" and introduced myself on Facebook as Maxwell Parker Donnelly. Max, because it sounded like my old nickname. (Plus, my grandmom's favorite coffee was Maxwell House!) Parker, honoring my mom's name. And Donnelly, for my dad's side, who I had recently connected with.

I used a quote from "Avengers: Endgame" to explain. As Frigga tells Thor, "Everyone fails at who they're supposed to be....The measure of a person, a hero, is how well they succeed at being who they are."

My announcement released a flood of love and support. Soon, my friends noticed that my confidence was skyrocketing. I've always been active in the community, using my talents in graphic design to help small businesses and nonprofits tell their stories, and now, I can do even more. I'm not spending my mental energy on playing the part of who I thought I was supposed to be. I can focus that energy on better things.

Take your time. Figure things out. Don't let yourself be locked into a single perception of yourself. No matter how hard others try to make you conform, be true to who you know yourself to be. Nobody can ever take that away from you.

Keep your chin up!
Max Donnelly

You know how in almost every group, there's the 'adorkable' dude who's always drawing cool stuff, thinks in pop culture references, and is basically a "lovable, droll geek?"

That's me!

I grew up in Philly and moved to southcentral Pennsylvania when I was almost 30. That's my sister's fault (she has a way of getting me into shenanigans...ask me about the 8-story high water slide). Then again, moving here probably saved my life, so...there's that.

"You were born with a spark that is uniquely yours."

Dear Friend,

You inspired the book you hold in your hands. That's right. You are an inspiration. Never forget that.

I was blessed with parents who did not teach prejudice to their children. If they had biases instilled in their childhoods, growing up in a coal mining region where identity was rooted in ethnicity and religion, they didn't act on them. And they didn't pass any to us.

The lesson I learned about LGBTQ people was, in fact, a positive one. My mother opened an antique shop when I was 15. She had never run a business before, but the idea came along, and with her usual energy and optimism, she made it a success.

She adored her regular customers, who delighted in the curious and quirky finds she stocked in the shop. Among them was a same-sex couple, and I will never forget the day she marveled at realizing that she enjoyed their company. She had never known any gay people before. These two taught her that any old fears were unfounded. They were good folks.

Those kinds of moments, the positive ones, are the lessons that made the biggest impression. As a teenager, it was dawning on me that my mother was not a judgmental person. She was even willing to rethink old notions. I absorbed those teachings like water soaking into my skin.

I have never understood the haters of this world, the people who twist grievance into their reasons for existence. If you are fortunate, you haven't encountered them. If they have inserted themselves into your life, I hope you have learned two of the primary lessons of this book. One, "clap back" at the first sign of bias. Don't give the bullies a victory. Two, find that tribe, that community, that family of choice that will elevate you above the doubters and detractors. It's hard. It's hard. It's hard, but they are looking for you. Once they find you, they will value your contributions and welcome you into their circle.

How to start? Use your talents and passions. If you read carefully, you'll see that every letter author who found a family of choice did so by following their dreams. They are artists and musicians and engineers and activists and administrators and public officials. You were born with a spark that is uniquely yours. Your job, now, is to fan it into a flame. Learn, study, practice, hone your talents.

Gold only shines when it's polished. The world is waiting for the gifts you have to share. As you build them into craft and expertise, your tribe will gather around and support you at every step along the way.

It has been my privilege and honor to edit this book. With every entry, I have found myself thinking of you - yes, you. Confident or scared, blissful or scarred, you have worth and so much to give. I admire your courage. I marvel - just like my mother - at your sense of humor and love for life. Go out and make this world better. We need you, and more importantly, as you follow your journey, you will find those who cherish you.

All my love,
Diane McCormick

Writing was in the stars for M. Diane McCormick since she got A+++'s on fourth-grade papers. Her degrees in writing, history, and journalism attest to her love for telling the real stories of real people. Diane is the editor of "How I Found My Pride" and author of "Well-Behaved Taverns Seldom Make History." She and her husband live in a circa-1910 home in Harrisburg, PA, with two cats who never lift a paw to help renovate.

CHAPTER 3

QUOTES

"When all Americans are treated as equal, no matter who they are or whom they love, we are all more free."

– President Barack Obama

CHAPTER 3

NOTES

....

....

....

....

....

....

....

....

....

....

....

....

....

....

....

....

....

....

"I had to do something, so I organized a vigil."

Dear You,

I grew up steeped in the culture of the Salvation Army. Everything I did and was taught to think was through this fundamentalist church. My earliest memory of what they wanted me to believe came during a van ride home from Sunday service. We drove through a neighborhood full of beautiful, rainbow-striped flags. I said I wanted one of those flags because they were so pretty, and a woman named Joan looked right at me and said, "You don't ever want one of those flags. Those people are going to hell."

So, at 5 years old, I was taught to associate gayness with sinfulness. The message never changed.

But I also remember a rainy day at summer camp when we watched "Mary Poppins," projected on a big bedsheet on the wall. The girls in my cabin talked about how cute Bert was, after that scene where the penguins pop out of the painting, and I said, "I'm gonna marry Mary Poppins. She's cute." And all the girls said, "Ewwwww. Chrissy's gay."

After college, I became a Salvation Army minister, until I was excommunicated for "chronic nonconformity." They said I let gay kids stay in the youth group, telling them they belonged there. They said that I was a joke and an embarrassment.

I felt awful. That kind of discouragement gets into your soul when it's reinforced for your entire life. I stayed firmly in the closet. It took five years before I could find my voice enough to say that I'm okay. Even then, I don't think I believed it, but I had friends who were willing to believe it for me.

I came out quietly, to friends and family on Facebook, but then the Pulse nightclub shooting happened, when a man killed 49 people inside one gay club. Something broke inside me, and it fixed something at the same time. I had to do something, so I organized a vigil. To my shock, 500 people turned out. I told the crowd that "we" had to pass a bill banning discrimination against gays in our town. That was all it took for my hometown newspaper to announce that I was gay.

We got that bill passed, but for a year, people said horrible things about me. It was a traumatic way to come out, and I never really had time to come to grips with it. I was so busy fighting for all of us that I didn't have a chance to focus on what my identity meant to me.

Fortunately, I was blessed to have those friends who were singing my song back to me. They saw the awesome person I was when I couldn't see it myself. That gave me the courage to finally say that I was ready to step into myself.

I'm getting married this year, to a wonderful partner who has come along on this wild ride of figuring out life. You often hear the phrase, "It gets better." Actually, that's only the beginning. When you can finally get to a place where you own your own power and your own story, your entire world shifts. You pop through that "Mary Poppins" painting, and you're dancing with the penguins.

Be who you are and don't be afraid to protect that, because who you are is a treasure. Find your family – maybe not the one you're born with, but the people who believe in you for you. They are the ones who will help you step into your power and step into your story.

All my love,
Chris

Chris Kapp is a Carlisle, Pennsylvania, writer and human rights activist who works as a homelessness and housing systems change specialist. She was ordained as a minister in 2002, after spending much of her final year of seminary working at Ground Zero in the aftermath of 9/11. The tireless advocate for LGBTQ+ rights founded the Carlisle Pride Week festival. Her original play "#IWillBeYourVoice: Stories of Homelessness and Hope" chronicles the true stories of homeless youth.

"All the lying and hiding was eroding my integrity."

My friend,

"And the day came when the risk to remain tight in the bud was more painful than the risk it took to blossom."

Writer Anaïs Nin said this many years ago. If you don't quite understand what she means, let me share my story. Maybe you, like me, will see yourself in this simple quote.

I grew up in a very conservative, Christian household where homosexuality was considered deplorable and a threat to everything good, pure, and wholesome. While the church I grew up in would preach love and acceptance for all, that did not translate into practice. My family loved me and meant well. I know they did their best to raise me as they believed was right.

Unsurprisingly, I was not exposed to different viewpoints and belief systems. When I graduated high school, I went to Bible College because we were taught that was the highest form of education.

I knew I was different in my teenage years, but I would never have admitted my sexual orientation to anyone. It wasn't until I met and fell in love with a woman in my early 20s that I realized that I could no longer deny my reality.

I spent several years living in denial and shame, firmly in the closet. I finally decided that all the lying and hiding was eroding my integrity to a point I could not tolerate. Coming out was a painful process in the beginning. I was struggling with an indoctrinated belief system which told me that who I was, was perverted and wrong.

I experienced the pain of losing relationships with many people that I loved and cared about. However, these pains did not compare to the inner pain I had been experiencing while being untrue to myself.

Are you starting to understand what Anaïs Nin said? "And the day came when the risk to remain tight in the bud was more painful than the risk it took to blossom."

I can now tell you, without reservation, that coming out and owning my truth and my identity was and continues to be worth it. I did experience loss, but I have gained so much. I have gained my chosen family. I have found a level of self-acceptance and confidence that I never would have thought was possible. I have found the love of my life, and we will be married.

In the beginning, I worried about the effect my decision to live as my authentic self would have on my career. I now see that being in a leadership role in healthcare as an out lesbian allows me to have a positive impact on my workplace and my community. I bring diversity to the table and give visibility to the LGBTQ+ community.

None of this would have been possible if I had allowed myself to remain trapped in self-loathing and shame.

We hear a lot about the importance of pride in the LGBTQ+ community. It was not until recently that I began to fully understand how important it is to embrace who we are and to celebrate both the unique differences and similarities of our shared experiences.

If you are struggling to accept yourself and fear the consequences of coming out, I want you to know that you are not alone. On the other side of this process is an inner freedom unlike any you have experienced. The more comfortable you are with yourself, the more other people will be, too. Please know that who you are is worth embracing and celebrating. You are destined to bloom, and that blossom will be beautiful.

In friendship and support,
Emily Taylor

Emily Taylor is a manager of several outpatient healthcare clinics in Camp Hill, Pennsylvania. She is passionate about helping people and promoting inclusivity and diversity in her workplace and community. She loves the beach and enjoys hiking and water sports. She loves to travel and have new experiences. She is excited to be starting the next chapter of her life with future wife and her dog, Shadow, in the Harrisburg, Pennsylvania, area.

"We filled the gaps in our lives."

Dear Friend,

Community. Friends. Family. Faith. A genuine life is one that entwines with others. Our story is a story about the power of togetherness.

Shannon's story: In many ways, I always knew that I was gay, even when I was too young to understand what that meant. Society was saying, "This is not something you should be championing." But I knew that perspective was wrong. After all, I didn't make this up. I knew how I felt inside.

I was fortunate, because my mom was open to letting me find myself. Plus, I went to a high school for the performing arts and found a community of friends just like me – all of us using our creativity to be our real selves.

I came out in phases, starting with my friends in my senior year of high school. It took another four years before I told my mom and grandmom. Their reaction: "Why did you wait so long?" The answer: You have to be ready. I was away at college in those years, growing maturity and confidence. I needed to present my complete self to the two people who meant the most to me in the world.

Emmanuel's story: I've always been loved and accepted, but that doesn't mean that I always felt comfortable. My dad was a small-town Mississippi boy who joined the Army. My mom came from Italy to marry my dad. I grew up in a conservative town in North Carolina. What else could we do but create our own community, where acceptance was the norm?

Outside of our cocoon, though, our church taught that homosexuality was a sin. I was left to wrestle with my feelings on my own. I turned my strengths to my advantage. I'm a thinker, so I thought. I researched. I prayed. In quiet times, I built a relationship with God and learned to understand my sexuality through faith.

"Wait a second," I thought. "If the Bible says I'm fiercely and wonderfully me, and all parts of me are a reflection of God, it's clearly the way that I was made, and maybe everyone else is misunderstanding."

My family had a hard time understanding, but my mom, especially, just didn't have the language of sexuality to have heartfelt talks. I figured that we would unpack things as life went on. Now, it's 15 years later, and my dad texts me every morning, and then he texts Shannon, like clockwork. And I'm pretty sure that my mom loves Shannon more than me.

Our story: We met here in Boston, through a dating app. In finding each other, we filled the gaps in our lives. Yes, we both have supportive families, but we're different from them, too. We both found that support person who truly understands what the other has been through. And we gifted each other with our individual networks of friends and colleagues. No one can go through this life alone.

Our advice:

• Get to the place where you understand the beauty and confidence in yourself, even if others refuse to see it.

• Find uplifting people and spaces so you can be your best self. How do you do that? Show up. Just show up. The universe will work its way to you if you meet it halfway.

• Lead with love. There's so much power when you fully understand what it means to love yourself.

We have been fortunate to find, after much searching, a powerful church family, in a historic Black church where the pastor is gay. Find the gems in every experience, he preaches. We leave his services thinking, "You know what? I can manage another week."

That's what this life is about. You change. You grow. You manage another week. Along the way, you find your best self and bond with all the other "best selves" who see the light in you.

All our love,
Shannon and Emmanuel Fairley-Pittman

"It is more than okay to be your complete and whole self."

Dear reader,

I am an ally.

Unfortunately, I would not have always defined myself as an ally. Growing up, I was never told that LGBTQ people were terrible or unholy or weird. But that's the thing. It just wasn't ever really discussed. I believe an ally is someone who completely sees a person of the LGBTQ population for the unique individual that they are and accepts every part of them.

An ally listens and offers support. An ally fights for what is right. Although I was never hateful (and my parents weren't either), I don't believe that I was doing enough to be called an ally until my adult years.

Looking back, I wish I would have advocated more for my queer classmates. I wish I would have challenged every time I heard someone say something derogatory to a queer classmate or say, "that's so gay." I wish I would have fought alongside those who demanded equal rights for gay marriage. I wish I would have reached out to my peers that were just coming out and let them know that I accepted them and supported them.

There are so many things I wish I would have done differently. So, as an ally, I am doing those things now.

To the sweet soul reading this book – I support you. I accept you. I deeply respect you.

I use and will continue to use my privilege to fight for you. I demand and will continue to demand equal rights and fair treatment for you. I will try my absolute hardest to influence the next generation for you. I will continue to teach my children for you and for future generations, too.

Dearest reader, it is more than okay to be your complete and whole self. The world is a better place with you in it.

We need more people to be authentic and genuine and true to who they are and how they feel inside, instead of maintaining a façade that is so completely out of touch with reality. We need you to be who you were meant to be and do great things. We need you to show the kids that come after you that it's okay to be who you truly are.

Actually, it's more than okay. It's beautiful. As Virginia Woolf said, "No need to be anybody but oneself."

Sending you so much love and light.

Love,
Danielle

Danielle Moran was born in Lancaster, Pennsylvania, grew up in South Florida and then returned to Pennsylvania in 2020. She has three children, Trey (7), Catalina, (5) and Joseph (2), and has been happily married to her best friend, Freddy, for nine years. Currently, Danielle is a counselor working with victims and survivors of narcissistic abuse as well as homeschooling her children.

"In the 21st century? Please."

Dear Friend,

When you hear the term "civil rights," what do you think of? Naturally, you're going to think of Martin Luther King, Jr., and the great Civil Rights movement of the 1950s and '60s. African-Americans marched, gathered, staged sit-ins, held boycotts, and even put their lives and freedom on the line in order to win the rights that belonged to them as U.S. citizens.

It was a stirring moment in history that ended in a sort of victory with passage of the Civil Rights Act of 1964, but the fight continues to win over hearts and minds still clinging to old prejudices. It was also a lesson in the importance of standing up against injustice, because as Dr. King himself put it, "Injustice anywhere is a threat to justice everywhere."

And here's where we get to the rights of the LGBTQ community. There was a time when being gay was characterized as a mental disorder. The historic Stonewall uprising of 1969 happened because gays and lesbians weren't going to tolerate legalized oppression anymore.

But again, the fight continues, all these years later. Queer Americans still face prejudice and stereotypes. As of this writing, 27 state legislatures still refuse to pass laws banning discrimination in housing, employment, and public accommodations based on a person's sexual orientation or identity. In those states, a landlord or employer can fire or evict someone – without consequences – simply because that person is LGBTQ.

In the 21st century? Please. That makes LGBTQ rights a civil rights issue, and it's why I create editorial cartoons for a newspaper covering LGBTQ issues. It started when I met the editor and had an idea. "Your newspaper needs a local cartoonist," I said. The editor and I think alike on the civil rights aspect of LGBTQ experiences. We share the mindset that cartoons can poke fun at society's old notions and all those people still lugging around their outdated prejudices.

It has to be done – using the power of images and a few well-chosen words to point out when people are being ridiculous or stubborn or selfish. We have made fun of churches, Congress, homophobes suppressing their own feelings, and businesses. In one cartoon, we showed a corporate board of directors stacked with LGBTQ members, but only 15 percent were out of the closet. Our point: There's always more than meets the eye. Hey, we will even challenge the LGBTQ community when political maneuvering and arbitrary divisions get in the way of progress. That's what editorial cartoons are for.

Drawing these cartoons empowers me to make a difference in our world, and that's the point of being an ally. Whatever talents we're given, we can put them to good use for the rest of society. How do we create a shift in the way the broader society thinks so that, finally, members of the LGBTQ community enjoy all the rights afforded them as citizens of the United States and the world?

I believe I play a part by sharing messages that are simple, humorous, and touch people in a way that make them think while they put smiles on their faces. That's also why I joined the board of my local LGBT center, especially to help raise funds for its crucial work. I connect people, and connections are the key to creating equal justice for marginalized communities. The more we can use our talents to fight for everyone enduring oppression in our world, the better off we all will be.

Keep up the fight,
Brad Gebhart

Brad Gebhart is development director for Hamilton Health Center in Harrisburg, Pennsylvania. He also is a member of the board of directors for the LGBT Center of Central Pennsylvania. Brad is active in the fine arts community as an artist, editorial cartoonist, and art teacher who serves on the board of the Art Association of Harrisburg.

CHAPTER 4

QUOTES

"This world would be a whole lot better if we just made an effort to be less horrible to one another."

– Elliott Page

CHAPTER 4

NOTES

....

....

....

....

....

....

....

....

....

....

....

....

....

....

....

....

....

....

....

....

"Am I really the gender I was assigned at birth?"

Dear Friend,

I grew up as the child of two gay dads in a Jewish household. Right away, you're thinking, "Well, that's different." And we were certainly very, very different from the norm. But I honestly didn't notice a difference.

I grew up believing that queer people had a place in Judaism. After all, one of my dads is a Reform rabbi, one of the first – if not the first – openly gay rabbis to graduate from rabbinical school. That was an important understanding in my life, and it helped me feel aware and equipped to come out as a lesbian.

But coming out later as trans was so hard that my memory has blocked out how I even became aware. I just know that I was a freshman in high school, struggling with the question of where transness fit in Judaism. It was like I had jigsaw pieces representing the two biggest parts of my life, but they were from different puzzles. They just didn't fit.

Fortunately, I found my community in Keshet, an organization for queer Jewish folks. Suddenly, I was meeting other Jewish queers. We talked about things like gender-neutral terminology in the Yiddish and Hebrew languages. I continue to work with Keshet to this day, running biweekly meetings for our young adult group. It's where I found my place, and now, I'm helping others find their place, too.

The first few months after I came out as trans were difficult, but by the first year, everything was good. We even joke now about how I chose my new name. I was listening to a lot of Pink Floyd in those days and felt like "The Dark Side of the Moon" fit my mood. I liked the sound of Floyd. It felt like me.

But one of my dads said, "Only old Jewish men are named Floyd! If you want to present masculine, what about Chuck or Joe?" Now, though, he likes my name. He grew into it, and he's probably the biggest trans supporter I know!

My senior year of high school was a time of transition. I wanted to be fully me when I entered college and adulthood. I legally changed my name and my Hebrew name. I had top surgery done.

I was fortunate to find a college with nongendered housing and where there's lots of queer programming, but I won't say that it's been entirely easy. I still get misgendered, so I've learned to take everything with a grain of salt. There will be ups and downs no matter what. You will be perceived by others differently no matter where you go.

If I could teach you one thing, it's that gender is a completely constructed factor. Think of gender as a consensual performance space. Am I really the gender I was assigned at birth, or am I just performing to live up to conventional expectations?

During the pandemic, people didn't have to "perform" their gender, right? So now, keep that feeling going. If you're into self-educating, there's always new queer theory to read and learn from. I loved "Fun Home," which my rabbi dad gave to me when I came out as a lesbian, and which was so important in helping me understand and realize my identity.

It's okay to not have a sense of self yet. It's okay to not understand fully where you are. There's no "deciding" that needs to happen. There are just feelings that you have. Have the confidence to find your happiness where you are, and happiness will find you.

Love,
Floyd Kessler

Hi, I'm Floyd. I use he/him pronouns, and I am a Jewish trans artist from Harrisburg, Pennsylvania.

"I'll have a job. Don't worry about me."

Dear Friend,

When you speak up for yourself and others, doors open to opportunity, friendship, and happiness. I know, because that is my story.

I grew up in 1950s-'60s Chicago, in a family that was devoted to social justice. My parents made sure that we had many different kinds of friends, which I didn't realize was highly unusual.

I realized I was gay when I was in high school. I was getting therapy, and the therapist said, "You don't want to be gay. You have to work on making sure that you're not."

And I thought, "Well, that's not going to work." I came out when I was 19, and my parents immediately embraced me and my life.

How could I know, at that moment, that my being gay would lead me down the path of becoming a spiritual leader in the faith I was raised in? You truly never know. I joined a synagogue with a strong gay and lesbian congregation and just naturally got involved. So did my parents! Many of my synagogue friends didn't have accepting families like mine, so my parents would invite them to our home for the Jewish holidays. Our table got bigger. Everyone had a seat!

Those were also, sadly, the days of the AIDS crisis. Some rabbis, priests, and ministers wouldn't perform funerals for people who died of AIDS. To me, this could not be. My whole life, I had been very much involved in knowing the Jewish liturgy, so I started performing funerals because nobody else would.

It's a very powerful thing to physically bury your friends. That's when I realized that I had to find a way to become a rabbi. In those days, of course, there were LGBTQ rabbis, but no one had ever been accepted in rabbinical school as openly gay. I became the first by stepping up as a strong advocate. I simply told the school, "It's really time for you to do the right thing."

They said, "No one will ever hire you." I said, "That'll be my problem." They said, "Are you going to spend all that money going to school for five years and not have a job?" I said, "I'll have a job. Don't worry about me."

I've been rabbi for my synagogue for 20 years now. Even in the early days, when members of a Pentecostal church picketed my synagogue's Friday evening services, my congregants stood by me, and they have always been very, very supportive. So much for not having a job.

Throughout all this, I lived my dream of being in a committed relationship and having a child. When our son, Floyd, came to me and said he was transgender, his other dad and I didn't try to tell him to wait a few years or ask if he was sure. I remembered my parents' example, and we said, "Let's figure out how to make sure you're happy."

I know that not all parents and friends are supportive, so my advice is: Be true to yourself. If you hit a brick wall in your journey to become whole, turn around and take a different path. There is always someone at the right spot who can mentor you and teach you that love is love. If your parents aren't supportive, what about your aunts and uncles? What about your grandparents? What about your teachers?

All of these good role models are out there. If you're stuck with one that isn't helpful, find one that's better. There are many paths to happiness and many paths to wholeness.

Shalom,
Rabbi Peter Kessler

Rabbi Peter Kessler has been Senior Rabbi at Temple Ohev Sholom in Harrisburg, Pennsylvania, since 2001. The native of Chicago received his B.S. degree in Business Management from the University of Illinois, master's and ordination from the Hebrew Union College-Jewish Institute of Religion, and Doctor of Divinity in 2021.

Rabbi Kessler is proud of his work in interfaith and community outreach and his vision for a congregation that is open and welcoming.

"I was tingly and giddy."

Dear Friend,

I was a late bloomer when it came to realizing that I'm queer. Even when I kind of knew, I misread the signs for a long time, but here I am - happy and comfortable in my queerness.

I grew up in a reform Jewish family, learning to value knowledge and to question everything. My mom was deeply into social justice, always protesting for women's rights and minority voting rights.

Family was the most important value I was raised on. I learned it from my dad. I also have an uncle who's gay, which I always knew and was super-comfortable with.

I was the girl who always had crushes on boys. Then I watched a show called "The L Word" - that's L for Lesbian - and I thought the lead character, Shane, was the coolest person ever. I couldn't believe I was attracted to a girl, but I justified it by saying she looked like a guy.

Then in college, one of my classmates reminded me of Shane, and I was crazy about her. I was still confused, though. What did it mean? I thought if I could kiss a girl, I'd know one way or the other. I went to a lesbian bar with my friends, and I wasn't going to leave that bar without kissing a girl.

You would think that wouldn't be hard, but it just wasn't working. Finally, I got that kiss and - nothing. I didn't feel anything inside. Same thing over the next couple of years whenever I tried to get close with anyone. I realize now they were just random women.

Then, after two years of pining for that classmate, we kissed, and it was a magical, magical kiss. I was tingly and giddy. I felt everything I thought I was supposed to feel.

So, lesson number one. Love makes a difference. It was the moment that turned things around for me. She and I never really dated, but I learned to date women and build good relationships. I went to Pride parties. I did all the fun stuff you associate with being gay.

Still, I hadn't told my family. I finally told my mom. She is so progressive, but she was shocked. We didn't talk about it in my house for a long time.

Lesson number two. Your parents want the best for you. From the second you're born, they dream about what your life will be like. If you tell them you're queer, they don't stop loving you, but they need to mourn the loss of your old self and learn to accept this new-to-them version of you.

Which my parents did. The first time my dad said anything about it, I was leaving for a teaching job in Bulgaria, and he said, "I want you to know I love you no matter what. I love everything that you are and every part of you. I want you to be happy, and I support you."

My message to you is, be patient, with yourself and with your family. This is not a race. Sexuality is a complex, changing thing. Just because you think you understand it today doesn't mean you'll understand it tomorrow.

Learn everything you can. Seek out queer mentors. Let your understanding develop in the way it needs to. Live your truth, and you will, like me, become part of a community that is beautiful and vibrant and loving.

Love,
Elyse

Elyse Krachman is an educator, a musician, a poet, and a storyteller who grew up in Northern Virginia. After teaching for a few years in Fairfax, Virginia, she moved overseas in pursuit of adventure and growth. Elyse currently lives in Munich, Germany, with her partner and is looking forward to one day adopting a dog.

"My home is a safe haven."

Dear Friend,

Transformation is an amazing thing. As you change, you grow. If you surround yourself with people who change and grow with you, you can do anything. I am an ally who transformed into a member of the LGBTQ+ community, and the journey has been amazing.

When I was growing up, my parents were heavily involved in theater. I ran up and down the aisles of our community theater. I played in the costume shop. I pretended to be a ticket taker in the lobby. I was surrounded by arts and enveloped by showtunes.

And as many theater communities do, they welcomed the gay community with open arms. I had never known my life to not have gay people in it. It was the norm to me. They were just some of the many warm, funny, talented people in my life. I never put a label on it, and neither did my parents.

As I grew older, it was only natural to align with the LGBTQ+ community. I started attending Central PA Pridefest. I was in my happy place because Tiffany was the headliner. Tiffany! (Trust me, kids. She was a sensation when I was your age.) After a few years, I became a volunteer and started bringing my daughter along. It was so important to show pride and solidarity with this loving community that I volunteered with the LGBT Center of Central Pa and then went on to work with the American Foundation for Suicide Prevention.

In 2018, our lives took a big turn. My daughter came to my husband and me, and she said, "Mom, dad...I'm queer. I just thought you should know." Were we surprised? No. But our feelings were indescribable! We were overwhelmed with pride that she felt safe enough to tell us her truth. That moment lit a spark inside me. I transitioned from fierce ally to fierce mama bear/ally and roared into action.

I joined Free Mom Hugs, that legion of moms determined to make a kinder world for their LGBTQ+ children, and got my shirt. I went to Pride and hugged everyone who approached me. That day turned me into Mama Bryden to all my daughter's friends. I fight for them the way I fight for my own. My home is a safe haven, and it will be a safe haven as long as this world harbors people who have hate in their hearts.

In 2020, I turned another corner. COVID locked us in our homes. With time on my hands to reflect, I looked back on the couple of years since I had turned 40, when I started noticing that I was drawn to certain women - women I met, women on television. I chalked it up to a "soul sister" thing, but when I was able to really sit down with these feelings, I realized there was nothing "soul vibey" here.

Could it be? Yes, it could. I was actually attracted to these women. In that moment, I became not only a fierce ally, but also a member of the community I so loved and fought for!

So, on September 23, 2020, I came out officially as bisexual. And it was really scary. But it also made me realize that there are more people full of love than full of hate. There are certainly reasons to be worried about coming out, but once you do it, you realize the good far outweighs the bad and that you are far from alone in this journey. This is a community, but this is also a family.

Love,
Bryden

Bryden McCurdy is a Harrisburg, Pennsylvania, native who lives with her husband, daughter, and two cats. She remains involved in theater, onstage and backstage. Bryden works as a customer service representative for a local insurance company. She loves reading and has set her sights on writing a book.

"He never told his story. I wish he could have."

Dear Friend,

Growing up in a poorer neighborhood of Harrisburg, Pennsylvania, was a memorable experience. There were neighbors who were very friendly, those who didn't speak at all, and those who I would see daily on their way to work, to shop downtown, to catch the bus out front of our home, or just walking through. As I reflect on my first experience or encounter with someone who seemed "different," it is the memory of this old neighborhood that comes to mind.

I can picture this scenario as if it were occurring at this very moment. The long, confident stride, the well put-together outfit, the glowing makeup, the "bobbed haircut" that bounced with every step. As if on cue, at certain times, neighbors could be seen on their porches or peering out their windows to get a glimpse of "Cupcake" making an appearance on Market Street.

Cupcake was the name she called herself by, and this is my earliest impressionable experience with someone who was proudly and openly gay. I was a young child, but recall thinking that yes, this person seemed out of the norm, but the impression that stayed with me was Cupcake's style and swagger. She walked like a model, each shoulder pushing forward with each stride. Even though the grown-ups seemed extremely amused by what they considered a spectacle, I admired that air of confidence.

In my early 20s, I was working for the state and had the good fortune to know a dear work buddy named Jim. He always looked so dashing, and he treated me with respect – never mind that I was a young, naïve Hispanic woman. He was funny as heck and taught me to take things in stride. If I had a bad day, it was Jim who would say, "Child, don't let it bother you." Then he would say savagely funny things about the people who were bothering me, and I would just have to laugh.

One day, Jim came to tell me that he had been let go from his job. "Why?" I asked through my tears. "Oh, you don't need to know," he said, as if he didn't want to burden me. He never told his story. I wish he could have. He didn't wear makeup like Cupcake, and he had a

52

beard, but he had the same inner confidence that I soaked up like a sponge. He instilled his pride in me.

So I wonder today, what if Cupcake could share her story? And what if Jim could tell his story? Therein lies the reason why it is important to not only read this book, but to consider how we can learn from these stories. The emotions and the passions of these heartfelt stories must have brought back painful memories for the writers. I truly believe, though, that sharing these stories for others to read will make a difference. I wish I could have read Jim's story, and Cupcake's, too.

And be sure, dear friend, to reach out to people who are going to support you, regardless. So many people have added value to my life. Cupcake didn't know it, but she did. So did Jim. He taught me tolerance and self-confidence. Even when he was going through bad times, he took time to help an inexperienced young woman.

These stories may be unique to the writers, but the experiences can resonate with each of us! The outcome will be in knowing that our friends, neighbors, and relationships can be enriched by the stories shared. Thank you all!

Respectfully,
Gloria Merrick

Gloria Vázquez Merrick is Executive Director of the Latino Hispanic American Community Center (LHACC) of the Greater Harrisburg (Pennsylvania) Region, empowering and advocating for the low-income Latino community. She attended HACC, Central Pennsylvania's Community College, and graduated with distinction from Eastern University. During her career in Pennsylvania state government, she led development of women's leadership capabilities and implemented statewide initiatives. She serves on several community boards and has won multiple awards.

CHAPTER 5

"Openness may not completely disarm prejudice, but it's a good place to start."

– James Baldwin

CHAPTER 5

NOTES

"Right there in Utah, I found a queer community."

Dear Friend,

"Oh, you're from Utah? Are you Mormon?"

Traveling around the U.S. and abroad, I have heard this question more times than I can count. Utah is more than religion, but the correlation is merited. I spent most of my youth immersed in Mormon culture, even when I wasn't a member. Religion wraps itself around you, your friendships, your family, your identify, and your daily life until you suddenly realize that it's suffocating you.

Where was positive queer representation? Nowhere, when you live in a community whose leaders put time and money towards keeping gay marriage illegal. I had supportive, loving parents, but nothing about my upbringing ever hinted that queerness was acceptable. When I was 13, the song "I Kissed a Girl" came on the radio, and my childhood best friend and her mother were disgusted by it. Their words hit me like a brick wall falling on my head. My feelings were that horrible? At that moment, I promised myself that I would hyper-focus on boys and shove down any girl crushes.

Inside, though, I started questioning everything the church was teaching me. I told myself, and even a friend I could share all of my doubts with, that I couldn't stand the church's stance on gay marriage. But of course, I was only an ally. (Did I have a HUGE crush on this friend? Yes. Would I admit that to myself? No way.)

When it was time to pick a college, I needed time and space to discover myself. So, my best friend and I packed our bags and moved four hours away, to southern Utah.

Here's the wonder of it all. Right there in Utah, I found a queer community and representation. Who knew? But there they were, in the women's rugby team and in Feminist Club. I even had a major crush on a teammate. As you know, crushes on women were nothing new to me, but this one was different – different because there was possibility. She was openly queer. Could a woman I was crushing on consider liking me? How terrifying, and thrilling!

Still, it took me another year to write down the word bisexual, and a few more months to come out to my friends. Even then, I felt as if my queerness wasn't "valid" somehow, as if "bisexual" was a label that people only used for attention. My past was covered in straight-passing privilege. I'd never even been in a WLW relationship. Wouldn't it be easier just to hide how I felt?

In time, I realized that my bisexual identify was valid. I am very privileged to have had so much support. For the most part, my parents and friends have been incredibly patient and loving. Out with all the guilt, imposter syndrome, insecurity, and shame! Occasionally, those feelings rear their ugly heads, but after years of self-reflection, exposure to positive representation, and feeling comfortable in my queerness, I know how to replace them with feelings of self-love and validity. I am in a loving, queer relationship with my partner. I have even reached the point where I am out to the students I teach.

Being out and proud every day can be difficult. Whether you come from a place that is full of support or drenched in oppression, being exactly who you are is a process. No matter where you fall on the LGBTQ+ spectrum, there are people with your same identify who not only made it through, but who will love you, support you, relate to you, and cheer you on. Know that there is hope.

Love,
Kristina

Born and raised in Ogden, Utah, Kristina Widerburg graduated from Utah State University with a degree in elementary education and a science emphasis. After graduating, she spent one year teaching English to students in Taiwan. The next year, she received a Fulbright grant to teach English in Athens, Greece. She currently lives in Salt Lake City, Utah, with her partner Faith, and loves traveling, yoga, writing, kayaking, and reading.

"I am strong despite their hurtful words."

To The Lovely Human Being Reading This Letter,

My name is Liam – but that was not always my name. I was assigned female at birth and raised as such in a conservative evangelical Christian family. I was taught that being gay was a sin. I did not even know what transgender was until I reached college. It all changed one day when I looked in a mirror, and that's what you'll learn about my story. Change does come, and it starts from within.

Back to the beginning. Despite my church lessons, I always knew something was different about me. As early as age 5, I truly felt like a boy. As I got older, my male friends couldn't come over for sleepovers, and I just could not understand why. When we lined up for lunch in two separate lines – one for boys and one for girls – I always felt that I should be with the boys.

As puberty hit, I started to feel alone. All my female friends were excited to get bras, put on makeup, and shave their legs. I only shaved my legs because, with my red hair, my classmates started to call me Orangutan. By the end of high school, I realized that I was attracted to women, but that only triggered a year of severe self-hatred due to my church teachings. The first time I kissed a girl (and LOVED it), I was so disgusted with myself that I cried for hours.

Still, realizing that I liked women seemed to make sense of how I'd always felt. In order to like women, you have to feel like a boy, right? I thrived in college as an out and proud lesbian.

But I still felt empty. Something was not right. Finally, one week before my 22nd birthday, I shaved my head and looked in the mirror. There, I saw my true self. In that moment, I knew. I was transgender. The boy I had always felt myself to be, had always known myself to be, was finally looking back at me.

You would not believe the love and support I experienced as I came out as transgender! My friends and extended family – my sister, aunts, uncles, cousins, and even all four of my grandparents – were behind me. Only my parents and other adults from my church reacted harshly. To this day, my parents do not call me Liam. It has been extremely painful to be without their unconditional acceptance and love, but it has made me who I am. I long to hear them say four simple words - "I love you, son" - but I know that I am strong despite their hurtful words.

Nowadays, I am five years on hormone replacement therapy. I have a deep voice, a full beard, and a flat chest thanks to top surgery. Lower surgery, aka "gender confirmation surgery," is next, and then I'll feel completely aligned within myself. As this physical transition draws closer, I am excited for the chance to simply live my life as me, free from the anguish of gender dysphoria - the disconnect between mind and body that many transgender people deal with.

I want you to know that there is happiness on the horizon when you embrace your truest self, whoever that may be, and allow yourself to be free. You are loved. You are valuable. You are special. You are YOU, and the world is so much better because you are here. If you think what I say next is cliché, think again. It is a simple truth: It does get better.

Love always,
Liam

Liam Magan lives in Keene, New Hampshire, and is happily married to his amazing and wonderful, non-binary spouse, Han. He has his own business doing septic system evaluations, though his true passion is in advocacy work - especially for the trans and queer community. He dreams of publishing a memoir, so stay tuned! He shares his journey across social media, and you can find a video diary of his entire transition on his YouTube channel.

"I deserved better than them. I deserved love."

Dear Friend,

I've known I was a lesbian since the fourth grade. It's a classic girl-meets-girl story. I moved to a new town in North Carolina, and on my first day of school, I met the other new student in my class. Her name was Meghan, and we became friends instantly. She listened to cool music, loved "Pirates of the Caribbean," and for some reason, she thought I was cool, too. I realized I might be different when one day, all I could think about was holding her hand. An innocent thing to do, of course, but I wanted to hold her hand the way Will Turner held Elizabeth Swann's hand when they were just about to kiss.

As the years went on, I did what every good Christian-raised, Southern girl does. I tried to shove those feelings as deep into my stomach as they would go. "Please stop feeling this way," I regularly uttered as I continued having secret girl crushes. The feelings did not go away. I had hoped that my crush on Zac Efron and the Jonas Brothers would be my saving grace. They all had long hair and sang like teenage mermaids. What's not to love?

But during my first semester of college, here came the real revelation. I realized I didn't need a saving grace! My university had an LGBTQ+ club called The Spectrum. It was led by a lesbian couple who were out and proud, and they were the first openly queer people I ever really met. I looked up to them and wanted to be just as out and just as proud.

Later that year, I met someone, too, and I knew I was ready to come out. My friends greeted me with overwhelming support. Coming out to my family, however, wasn't so nice. I left my mom a letter and vacated the premises for the weekend. I had heard stories about people getting into fights and saying things they later regretted, and I did not want that to happen. Unfortunately, after the weekend, no discussion was had. She was overwhelmed with anger and disgust, I would later learn. As my life continued, fights were had, lines were drawn, and eventually, I'd had enough. I deserved better than them. I deserved love.

I have always been able to surround myself with loving friends and supportive people. I've never felt like the odd woman out, and I've always had a friendly home to spend the holidays in. I could not have a better life. Over the past few years, I have grown to love and accept myself fully. I am doing all the things I never thought possible as a queer person. I met my girlfriend abroad, and we settled down. We are very close with her family, and they are extremely loving and supportive.

I am so hopeful for what lies in store. The world is full of terrible things, but wonderful things too. I cannot wait to get married, settle down, and build the family I never had. All of this is possible for you, too. You deserve love and acceptance, and don't ever let anyone tell you different.

If you don't feel strong now, that's okay. There's nothing wrong with you. Nothing at all. You are beautiful, creative, loving, inspiring, and DESERVING of all the things this world has to offer. You are loved by your friends. You are loved by your chosen family. You are loved by me. You are so loved. You are so loved. You are so loved. You are so loved. I promise, you are so loved.

All my love,
Faith

Born in West Virginia, Faith Brown moved up and down the East Coast until recently settling down in Utah. She taught English in Bulgaria on a Fulbright grant and worked for an international educational nonprofit. Those experiences led to her passion for helping students achieve their goals through academic advising. She enjoys reading, kayaking, playing with her cat, cuddling with her girlfriend, and pretending she knows how to sing and dance.

"Being myself opens doors."

Dear Friend,

An immigrant learning a new language and new culture. A homeless child living on the street. A child watching his mother escape domestic violence and work multiple jobs to provide for her children. A boy who knew he was not the macho heterosexual his family expected him to be.

I was, and still am in my heart, all of these things, but they didn't wear me down. They are the fuel that drives my passion to be my true self and to help others overcome their own challenges.

When we emigrated to the U.S. from the Dominican Republic, I was 8 years old. I went from a middle-class life and private schooling to city living and public schools. My mother married a man who abused her. When she left that relationship, we found ourselves living on the street.

That's when the YMCA took us in. The Y became a passport for my mom into an independent life with a home and a car. I will never forget the wonderful things they did for us.

Through all this, I knew that I was "not normal." I come from a very macho Latino family. My uncles and aunts would urge me to check out a girl or ask whether I had a girlfriend, but I was checking out boys at the gym. The kid with the rolled-up sleeves on his t-shirt was cute. Still, I kept fighting it and fighting it.

I was 18 when I grew the grit to do what I had to do. People were starting to talk. My mom needed to hear the truth straight from me, and not from the rumor mill.

So I wrote her a letter. I apologized for not being the man she wanted me to be. For the next seven years, we talked. We asked questions about what made each other uncomfortable. We listened. Most importantly, we showed respect, even when we disagreed.

And one day, she woke up and said, "I love my son. I don't care what you are. I will forever love you. You are so special to me." Today, she sees my partner as another son. When I call her, the first thing she asks is, "How's Nelson?"

Truly, there is light at the end of the tunnel. I am living my dream. When I was a boy, I saw my mom struggling because she couldn't connect the dots to find help. So, I founded a company to make those connections for low-income people and people of color. We are passionate about helping people step over their barriers and lead healthier lives.

If I had never come out, I would not have been successful. I would never feel the gratification of making a difference in the lives of others. Being myself opens doors. I'm able to openly say to the CEO of a health care company, "I'm Latino. I'm gay. I know how to reach these communities because I've lived through their struggles."

If you're struggling, get help from someone you can trust. In Latino families, for sure, there's always that one aunt or uncle who just knows. Talk to that tía or tío, or find some other trusted adult. They will become your champion and help you along the way.

Wonderful times are ahead if you embrace your authentic self. Others will see your honesty. They will join you in making the world a better place, and you will feel happy and fulfilled. When you shake off the fear and let your passion be your guide, you can do anything.

All my love,
George

George Fernandez, of Harrisburg, Pennsylvania, is CEO of Latino Connection, the community education and health outreach dedicated to empowering and uplifting the Latino community. The experiences of his mother, a single mother of three and victim of domestic violence, inspired him to create Latino Connection, "to ensure that Latino and non-white communities never experience what my family did and always have adequate access to social assistance programs, education, and resources," he says.

"You are not alone, and never have been."

To my dear queer friends,

One of the most important things to know when you are going through something difficult is: you are not alone.

When discovering your identity as a queer or trans person, you might feel as though no one can understand you, as though everyone you know lives on a different planet or speaks another language and could never understand or empathize with your experience. I know I felt that way when I began to explore my own sexuality in college, and discovered that it was more complex and broad than I initially thought. This discovery was scary and I felt alone, like none of my friends or relatives would understand. I still feel that way sometimes.

But years later when I began studying to become a rabbi, a leader of a Jewish community, I learned from Jewish tradition that many of the hardships we go through today were shared by our ancestors in every generation. When we feel alone and lost, when we feel pain in our relationships, our bodies, or our hearts, we can look to the wisdom of our ancestors who experienced these things before us and find help.

Those who study Jewish tradition, which is thousands of years old, can find evidence of queer and trans people living in every era. The rabbis who lived between the years 100 and 500 of the common era spoke about many different kinds of genders, including male, female, those who are both, those who are neither, and more.

Some references to gay and trans identity are obvious, while some have to be read between the lines. Some people who read the bible understand that King David and prince Jonathan were not just friends who made a pact but lovers who made a romantic vow. The book of Samuel says, "When [David] finished speaking with Saul, Jonathan's soul became bound up with the soul of David... Jonathan and David made a pact, because [Jonathan] loved him as himself. Jonathan took off the cloak and tunic he was wearing and gave them to David, together with his sword, bow, and belt." (1 Samuel 18:1-4) Later, when Jonathan dies, David says, "I grieve for you, My brother Jonathan, You were most dear to me. Your love was wonderful to me, more than the love of women." (2 Samuel 1:26)

Some people read the bond between Naomi and Ruth as romantic, too. Ruth says to Naomi, "Do not urge me to leave you, to turn back and not follow you. For wherever you go, I will go; wherever you lodge, I will lodge; your people shall be my people, and your God my God." (Ruth 1:16)

Some are obvious and some are hidden, but wherever you look there are stories of gay and trans people. Rabbi Benay Lappe, a lesbian Jew who started a special school for queer study of Jewish text, calls them "donkey stories." If donkeys could read the bible and rabbinic text, they would notice so many stories about donkeys! The same goes for people. We read through the lens of our experience, and can therefore find lots of stories about people like us, including queer and trans people.

So the next time you feel alone, read carefully whatever you are looking at. Whether it's the bible, a textbook, a novel, or a magazine - you may find stories, both in the text and between the lines, showing you that you are not alone, that there are people and have been people just like you throughout the world, for all of time, surviving, loving and living beautiful lives.

With love,
Rabbi Ariana Capptauber

Rabbi Ariana Capptauber is the rabbi of Beth El Temple, Harrisburg, Pennsylvania, where she lives with her spouse, Baruch, and her baby, Yonah. Previously, Ariana lived in New York City and then White Plains, New York, while studying at the Jewish Theological seminary, where she was ordained in 2020. Ariana loves to read and write fiction, hike and be outdoors, travel around the world, fight for social justice, and play with her family.

"We should indeed keep calm in the face of difference, and live our lives in a state of inclusion and wonder at the diversity of humanity."

– George Takei

CHAPTER 6

NOTES

....
....
....
....
....
....
....
....
....
....
....
....
....
....
....
....
....
....
....

"This is the family that I choose."

Dear Friend,

Sometimes I think my story is cliché, like the plot of all those movies where the main gay character isn't accepted by his or her religious parents.

But people tell me that my story is actually quite remarkable. I guess it's because I turned moments with friends – and one amazing moment, in particular – into life lessons about who your family really is, and how to make your life about a happy future and not about any unhappiness you might be feeling now.

Here's the backstory. I was born in a large, Catholic family. My father is a deacon, and the family goes to church every Sunday.

In the movies, the gay character is usually ashamed of their sexuality, but I was so young when I realized I was gay that it rarely occurred to me to be ashamed. I didn't, and still don't, have a problem being a boy who likes other boys, but my religious background made it hard for me to feel proud.

In 2015, when gay marriage was legalized in the U.S., my father preached at Sunday mass about how gay people were "ruining the institution of marriage." For months, he would preach that being gay was a sin. No, it wasn't the first time that I had experienced homophobia, but wow. Here it was in my own family, harder to take than any bullying I had endured. A rift was growing between me and my family and church. I thought that the only way to mend it was to retreat into the closet and change who I was.

In my freshman year of high school, I came out to my parents. My mother told me that I was unlovable and that I was making a mistake by "choosing" to be gay. She threatened to kick me out of the house. By then, I had heard every homophobic argument against my right to exist, and they were starting to sound like a sad, overplayed song. I felt an ache, of course, at my parents overtly rejecting me, but it was a dull ache.

I had to seek support and comfort outside of my family, so I reached out to friends. I lost people very close to me, but I became closer with those who truly accepted me. Then there was the day that a friend and coworker named Emily told me a story. It was her coming-out story and how she came to realize that she was bisexual. That's when it hit me. Here was an adult presence in my life who was not just queer, but actually living a happy, fulfilling life.

What a revelation! For the first time, I realized I was not alone and that I had a future beyond any hardship or pain I was experiencing in that moment. What I'm going through at any given moment does not determine where I will go. Having that support, especially from an adult, has meant the world to me.

I have found friends, peers, and role models who help me through the dark periods. They listen. Many have gone through similar experiences. This is the family that I choose, and you can do the same. Related or not, they will be there to support you and help you find hope in the most hopeless situations.

There are people ready to welcome you with open arms and love you for who you are. It is a privilege to have found my chosen family. I urge you to find yours. There will always be someone in the world ready to love you for who you are.

Love,
Theodore

Theodore Heil was born and raised in Pennsylvania. He spends most of his time writing, reading, and playing with his two cats.
When he is out of college, he wants to move to New Jersey and eat breakfast on the beach. You can find him at his local library or on Twitter @theodreh.

"My mother stepped up and supported me."

Dear Friend,

The journey continues...

During my childhood, I was faced with many challenges. However, I was raised by a hardworking, single mother of four. She did her best to instill the value of a good education, ensure we had a stable home, and promote self-expression.

I was surrounded by a largely Catholic religious environment. My mother was Lutheran, but I attended a non-denominational church headed by Catholic priests. While I was taught to follow religious ideals of faith, my mother also made sure I was exposed to other churches, community organizations, and sports.

All these opportunities became outlets for growth, and even at a young age, I started to realize I was different. I became attached to friends more than usual. I knew there was something out of the norm.

I got more involved in church groups, community events, and camps as a volunteer and participant. I thought I just had to get my mind off any feelings that didn't seem "normal" or in line with what I was supposed to be doing. I felt others were judging me, even friends. I believed I shouldn't be having these thoughts or invest too much time in them.

During middle school and high school, I experienced feelings of attraction towards a friend that were more than platonic, more than "just friends." I didn't know what this meant, and it became weird. It was difficult for me to find any support or someone understanding of my feelings.

Trying to date boys in high school didn't go anywhere. I managed to push those feelings away and focused on school, extracurricular activities, and my part-time job. My first kiss with a same-sex person wasn't until I was 20 years old, and I was 25 when I finally pursued same-sex relationships.

As for my mom – well, she "knew," or at least had an idea. How did I finally come out to her? It's kind of funny. I visited with a "friend from college" – who was obviously gay. That started a gradual process of dialog and acceptance.

At first, my mom thought it was a phase that would wear off. She wondered if there had been a bad experience or some "reason" that drove me to this. I would explain my feelings and how I feel more natural being with the same sex. I truly opened up to her about my same-sex relations vs. opposite-sex relations.

All that dialog helped me wrap my brain around this, too. In time, we both realized this was a permanent way of life rather than a mere choice. My mother stepped up and became very supportive. As long as she was on my side, I had the confidence to feel more comfortable around everyone else.

I looked around and realized that many friends who supported me already knew. Other friends and family members didn't agree with my newfound lifestyle. To be honest, I wasn't even sure this was the right path for me. Sometimes, they had me confused, but it helped to find others I could speak to or go to for advice.

The thing to remember is this: It's STILL a journey. It's ALWAYS a journey. While I continue to love myself for who I am and embrace my differences, I also have learned to embrace the journey. Take time in finding yourself. Nothing is easy in life, but pushing away or being ashamed of your true self is not the way toward self-actualization. The journey towards complete self-acceptance, self-confidence, and self-love is just as enjoyable as growing into your true self and fulfilling purpose.

Much Love,
Jaime

Jaime J. Johnsen is a long-time resident of the city of Harrisburg, Pennsylvania, and currently works as a hospitality service director. She is a current elected candidate for Harrisburg School Board Director. Formerly employed by Harrisburg City Government as a proud Union member, she helped to develop and implement the 311 system. A proud HACC transfer student, she continued her education at Penn State Harrisburg, majoring in Psychology, studying Sociology and Child Development. Jaime previously served on the executive board of the Dauphin County Young Dems and the Capitol Region Stonewall Democrats. Currently, Jaime is an active member of the Federation of Democratic Women and continues to be involved in a number of community organizations and nonprofits in Harrisburg.

"And she chose love."

Dear Friend,

Life is a blessing. There will be bumps along the way, but my story shows that you can envision the future you want and then make it happen.

I don't have much "baggage" from childhood. There were name callings, and I didn't like that, but I always knew I was different, truly from as far back as I can remember. I never fooled myself into thinking that I could change. I was always aware of who I was.

I came out in college, when a friend drove me to a gay bar and said, "Surprise! I'm gay." And I said, "Well, me too."

It was so simple. It was freeing. I came out to friends, but my parents still didn't know. One weekend after I graduated, I visited them with someone I was dating. They didn't know this, but things were uncomfortable. Later, my mom asked me three times, "Are you gay?" Finally, I said, "Yes."

Moms just know, but she needed to hear it. Things were strained with my family for the next few months, but one day, my mother told our family doctor that I was gay. He said, "Mrs. Davis, I know." He talked her through her feelings. He said, "Mrs. Davis, love him or lose him."

And she chose love. She wanted me only, she said, to be safe. From then on, my mom and I were never closer. My dad and I never spoke about it, which was okay. But then came an unspoken moment. I was in a relationship with someone my parents liked. My parents and his agreed to help finance a house we were buying, and my parents came to see the place. As they were leaving, I said to my dad, "I love you," He wasn't the type to say that out loud, but he said, "I love you, too."

So he accepted. And that was the last time I saw him. He died a month later. The lesson I learned is that you can't force anyone to accept you and your life. They have to come around, whether it's about your sexuality, or getting divorced, or anything else. You just have to give it time.

Let me share a story of how life comes full circle. After I came out, I made some friends who were all gay men and about 10 years older than me. We often gathered for brunch on Sunday mornings. We would eat quiche – oh, my gosh, I had never eaten quiche – and I loved those days. I would think, "I have a whole lifetime of this to look forward to." I looked forward to being them – being in my 30s, having my own place, maybe having a relationship, having stability.

About 20 years later, I was on vacation with my now-ex, and we stopped for brunch at that same restaurant. Maybe I was sitting in that same seat. The memories of those guys came flooding back, and it came to me. I've had that life, the one I hoped for. It was like going back to your birthplace, which in a sense, it was. I was looking forward and backward at the same time, and having no regrets.

I don't take my story for granted, because I've lived a blessed life. I just like to think that I've given my town a recognizable face of the LGBT community who has been a nice guy and helped a lot of people.

So that's my advice. Find satisfaction where you are. Be who you are first. The rest will follow.

In sincere friendship,
Ray Davis

Ray Davis was born in 1954, in Bethlehem, Pennsylvania – a true "Baby Boomer"! He attended Catholic school for 12 years before majoring in ornamental horticulture at Delaware Valley College. He moved to Harrisburg in 1986 and began selling real estate in 1992. Currently single, he has had two long-term relationships. He adores his family – two sisters, six nephews and nieces and six "greats". Bella, his Welsh Terrier, is his constant companion.

"I see so much pain behind your eyes."

Dear Friend,

When I was younger, I owned stacks of Barbie dolls - the ones my wonderful grandmother bought for me at yard sales. There they were, beside the first CDs I ever owned. Britney Spears. Shania Twain. The "Grease" soundtrack.

I mean, really? How could I have missed the signs? If I had known then that I was gay, I could have been so much more accepting of myself. But you can't beat yourself up about what you missed. When the time is right, the real you will emerge.

Like so many people, I grew up in a small town. When my family became involved in a church, I heard the messages. Being gay was a sin. If it was against God's will, I thought, I must not be gay.

Maybe that's why I pushed away my feelings. Still, I was curious, and I'd search the internet. I'd see images of men, and I'd think, "This is different, but I like it."

I went to college, and boy, did I stretch myself thin, with classes, working, and fraternity life. In the middle of all this, I met a boy online, and he was supercute. We talked, and he told me he was gay. He was the first person to say, "I see so much pain behind your eyes."

Maybe I needed someone to open that door. I didn't know him that well, but he was the first person I came out to.

When it was time to fully come out, there was no question who would be first. My parents and I always shared everything going on in our lives. I woke up one morning and thought, "Today." Just as they were putting the leash on our dog for their daily walk, I said, "Mom, Dad, I have something to tell you. I think I'm bi."

They looked at each other and said, "That's gonna give us something to talk about on our walk."

When they came back, they said, "Nothing has changed. We still love you."

Still, there was an adjustment period. Maybe I knew things had changed when my parents met Jorge, my boyfriend, at my dearest friend's wedding (I was her "gay of honor"). Jorge was staying at our home, and my dad had insisted that we sleep in separate rooms.

But after my dad saw us together at the reception, just being ourselves, he came over and said, "You know what? You guys can stay in the same room." I saw it as an olive branch. My dad is a "manly man," but he has his way of showing love and acceptance.

Here's the kicker. When we got home that night, Jorge said we would sleep in separate rooms. "I want to show them respect like they showed us respect," he said.

Respect. When you give it, it comes back to you. Jorge and I are married now, and my parents love him! Just remember that the journey takes time. After all, you're not just working through your sexuality. You're also figuring out how to be an adult. That's universal. Everyone needs time to find the person inside.

While you're searching, don't let social media make you feel inferior. So many LGBTQ people struggle with body image because we see these perfect, muscular bodies everywhere. I've worked my career in graphic design, and I know those images are just a product someone is trying to sell you.

Instead, use the power of social media to find your community. Reach out to the people who will see and love the authentic you. Take their affirmation, and remember that the only person you need to impress is you. You are your number one fan!

Love,
Kyle

Kyle J. Pinto-Malinosky is pursuing his career in graphic design and theater. In November 2020, Kyle married the love of his life. They live in Lancaster, Pennsylvania, with their cat, Clementine. They plan on moving to New York City for their next great adventure! To all the readers of this book, they dedicate this letter to you, to know that you are loved and there is a special place for you in this wonderful and ever-changing world. XO

"I still do not know if my face showed my shock."

Dear Friend,

The truth can set you free ... painfully. I have been a defender of the downtrodden. I have fought for those "weaker" than me. I have befriended those laughed at, scorned, rejected. I have defended the rights of all people to live freely, except...

Raised in the church, I had parameters around what "free" meant. From early childhood, I learned homosexuality was a sin. One man/ one woman. Anything else was either an abomination to God or sinful. I was also taught to love my neighbor as myself. Yep. Mixed messages made life uncomfortable.

Somehow, I decided as long as I did not directly discriminate against another person, I was still doing the right thing. I could hold fast to my religious beliefs and secretly call persons sinners or lost if they identified as Lesbian, Gay, Bi-Sexual, Trans, Questioning, Queer (LGBTQ+), or any of the other identities within the + sign, such as non-binary, fluid, etc. I was unable, however, to reconcile how a person could be intersexed.

Having gay, trans, and bi relatives and friends helped, but I wanted to understand what God had to say about the intersexed. My interpretation of scripture needed to answer the most difficult question, or it would all fall apart. I had to find an answer for the multi-sexed in order for me to find an answer for how I was supposed to respond to the societal challenge of the LGBTQ+ community. (I'm sharing my journey. It doesn't have to make sense.)

A cousin I played with as a child born male had become a female and married! It took a while for me to digest that one. She is so beautiful in her willingness to talk with me. I still find myself wondering about her life's navigation.

Several good friends and bonus children who freely explored their sexuality would talk with me as if it was normal for me to be with people who did so. I still do not know if my face showed my shock or if I did a good job of hiding my confusion.

Finally, a friend, Joli Iensuo, who is queer and non-binary, came into my life, and one of their many skills is educating others about "holistic safety and wellness of sexuality and gender expansive people." They created an organization, Root Rise Consulting, and work with individuals, corporations, and organizations to help create safer space for all. Joli answered my questions without making me feel stupid or hypocritical. Their friendship, and that of their entire family, has made a huge difference in my understanding.

There is an old proverb, "when the student is ready, the teacher will come." For me, it remains a process. I have made HUGE mistakes along the way. While never knowingly discriminating against any employee or colleague, I have been insensitive.

On one hand, I was friendly with people who identified as LGBTQ+ and defended them, but I also made insensitive comments when they weren't around or snickered at someone's looks or demeanor. I cannot undo my mistakes. Nor have I thrown all of my beliefs out of the window. I find myself holding fast to one – to love my neighbors as myself. Every person has the right to be treated with respect and decency, and to be able to work for their dreams.

If you need me to stand with you, I will. I may be uncomfortable and out of my element, but I will stand with you – not because I understand your journey. I will stand with you because I understand mine.

With you along the way,
La-Verna Fountain

La-Verna Fountain, https://IAmLJFountain. com, is the founder of Meaningful Communications Matter LLC, focusing on bridging the divide of misunderstandings in the home, community, and workplace. In 2018, she retired from Columbia University, where she served as Vice President for Strategic Communications and Construction Business Initiatives. She is a U.S. Army veteran and community volunteer. La-Verna and her husband of 40 years, James, live in Pennsylvania and would be empty nesters except for their large, spoiled German Shepherd.

"People who love each other and want to live together should be able to enjoy the blessings and the strife of the marriage relationship."

- Justice Ruth Bader Ginsburg

CHAPTER 7

NOTES

"I buy all the rainbow stuff I can find and wear it proudly."

Dear Fabulous Friend,

In a tall kitchen window of my home, there's a big, pastel, rainbowy sign. It says, "All are welcome." As an ally and fiercest of fierce mama bears, I mean that. If you arrive at my door, you are invited in. And if you can't make it here, please know that you are welcome in my heart, and that there are others out there like me ready to fill your life with love.

How did I get this way? Well, I love everyone – and especially my son, Sean. He is 23 years old, my firstborn. I can't even imagine not loving him because he is gay. The day it became apparent was the day that we were worried that he was being bullied and didn't want to tell us. After what seemed like forever, I just blurted out, "Is this about your sexuality?" He still wasn't ready to tell us. Finally, I asked, "Are you gay?"

"Yes," he said. And that was that. It was a conversation that changed absolutely nothing about the love we feel for my patient, smart, humble, conscientious, kindhearted boy. My husband told him that he could be a purple alien but that he is our son, and that is all that matters.

I research everything I can about the LGBTQ+ community, just so I can stand with Sean. And I learn so much, too! Once, at a Pride festival, I was looking for a bear sticker to show I am a mama bear, and a kind person gently explained that not all bears stand for the same thing. We both laughed and realized that what I wanted was a rainbow bear sticker that said "mama" on it.

I am such a proud ally that old friends who've seen my Facebook posts have asked for advice on dealing with their own children. Love is love, I tell them. Love them even harder. It's as simple as that. It helps to show that we parents have a story, too, and that we are in this forever with our children. Each of my children is special. Both my daughter and son like boys, so how cool is that? As long as they bring home decent human beings, I am happy. Good attracts good, so I think we'll be okay.

Sean isn't a big fan of rainbow capitalism, and much to his chagrin, I buy all the rainbow stuff I can find and wear it proudly. I don't even have a favorite piece. EVERYTHNG rainbow is my favorite! I just can't get enough. I love wearing rainbows and unicorns as a small way to show that I am an ally.

One of the highlights of our family life was being in Ireland with my daughter's Irish dance school, and learning that the Dublin Pride Parade – historically, one of the world's first – was going on. Well, of course, we joined in! What a coincidence, and what great memories we have simply because our family is open to sharing Sean's journey!

I know that not every young member of the LGBTQ+ community is fortunate to have a loving family, but I assure you – there are people out there who will love you for who you are. Do the things that you're passionate about, and those generous souls will find you. Make a place in their lives, and I promise, they will make a place for you in their hearts.

All my love,
Leigh-Ann Reitze

Leigh-Ann Reitze is senior events planner for UPMC in Central Pennsylvania. She is responsible for ensuring every event runs smoothly, that all attendees are fully engaged, and UPMC is well represented in the community and the organizations it supports. She also supports UPMC's strategic relationships, coordinates volunteers, and collaborates with local corporate partners. Leigh-Ann is also passionate about her involvement with many community causes. She holds a bachelor's degree from Mansfield University.

"I discovered an inner strength."

Dear Friend,

Any story about my life begins with a simple statement. I am a pastor's kid, born in Philadelphia, raised in the church, and taught to follow my family's traditions and not make waves. That may be how it began, but even in my earliest years, I found myself willing to challenge my belief systems, ask questions, and experience as much in life as possible.

I was brought up believing that being gay was wrong, sinful, and would lead me straight to hell. It was a terrifying notion – especially as I began to understand more of who I really was. My journey to acceptance was challenging, and it led me to Central Pennsylvania when I decided to attend Messiah College.

Many people struggling with their sexuality also struggle to reconcile it with their faith, and I was no different. But, in what seemed like a terribly long process, I came to realize that my faith was secure, that my authenticity as a person mattered more than anything else, and that living my truth brought much more freedom, not less.

All these words make it sound so much easier than it was, but it was hard. I lost relationships and strained others. My family struggled with my coming out, to the point where my Dad and I did not speak for over 10 years. However, through that pain, I discovered an inner strength that I didn't know I had, and that strength has carried me through some of my most difficult challenges.

At one point, I thought I would have to move away from my new hometown of Harrisburg to find community, but I was wrong. I found a community of support that became my foundation and the reason why I have been so grounded here. Our "family" is far more than bloodlines, I realized. It is about your chosen family, and mine has been instrumental in my journey to acceptance.

My inner strength has led me to a successful career devoted to human resources and coaching organizations to create safe places for all people to work. I have created inclusive policies for companies to ensure that every employee receives a fair shot regardless of sexuality, gender, gender identity, race, country of origin, or any other characteristic that makes them unique and authentic.

That strength also led me to run for and win a seat on Harrisburg City Council, where I was able to champion the under-represented. In 2018, I was honored to be appointed by Pennsylvania Gov. Wolf to serve on the Pennsylvania Commission for LGBTQ Affairs, the first statewide commission of its kind in the nation.

My work and public service have created a platform that allows me to spotlight the needs and issues of the LGBTQ community. I have passed legislation that shed light on the harmful effects of conversion therapy on LGBTQ youth, and I continue to advocate for legislation that would ban discrimination against the LGBTQ community.

My advice is simple. Always remember that you are loved as your authentic self, and never let anyone tell you otherwise. On this journey through life, you will meet amazing people who will love and accept you for who you are, and they will become your friends and chosen family. I hope you will find love and happiness as I have by living both openly and authentically. The greatest moment in my life was to walk down the aisle with the love of my life, in front of our friends and family, declare our vows and be able to loudly affirm that love always wins.

Be true,
Ben Allatt

Ben Allatt is an executive and public servant based in Harrisburg, Pennsylvania. He is a consultant with Alternative HR, where he works with clients on building, maintaining, and growing their human relations functions.
From 2014 to 2020, he served two terms on Harrisburg City Council, including one term as vice president. In 2020, he began his second term with the Pennsylvania Commission on LGBTQ Affairs. Ben lives in midtown Harrisburg with his husband, Stephen.

"She thanked me for opening her heart and her mind."

Dear Friend,

Maybe you're struggling like I did to see where you fit into your world, but I can tell you what makes the difference. Own your wonderful self, and educate others about who you are.

I was raised in a Christian household. I was the "tomboy" because I liked to hang with the guys playing sports. I was baptized as a Seventh Day Adventist, so we went to church every Saturday, practically from sunup to sundown. I was raised to believe that homosexuality was bad.

And yet, I always felt inside that I was different. I never was the type to follow the crowd, but because homosexuality was frowned upon, I was afraid to speak my truth. I was living in secrecy because I didn't want to be looked at as the black sheep of the family.

Fortunately, I also had an inner strength. I just knew that I was special, like a superstar. I've always felt like I was going be on TV and leave an impact on the world in a positive way. I have always felt legendary. I had so many gifts growing up. There was nothing I couldn't do. One week I was playing basketball, and the next week I was playing the drums.

It was basketball that finally helped me break my silence. I was playing basketball for an all-female league, but I had to change out of my basketball clothes at home because "that's what a lesbian would wear." My mother didn't want me looking "like a little boy."

It was rough and challenging trying to express myself to my mother until I decided to own my truth. I looked in the mirror and said to myself, "If my mother loves me, she will have to learn to love me regardless - flaws and all." I told myself that I have to live my honest truth and that what's inside of me is what makes me happy.

So, I did just that. I owned who I am. I owned all of me and everything that comes with me. Then, I sat my mother down. I fully explained how I felt on the inside and said that, if she loves me, love is unconditional. I explained to her that as a single parent, she had done an incredible job of raising me, and that my sexuality or sexual preferences had nothing to do with anything.

I educated my mother on what was happening in my life and on what I was feeling. More than anything, I said, I needed her support and love.

It took some time, but eventually she fully understood and accepted me for who I am. My mother is now one of my best friends, and she supports me in every way possible. She thanked me for opening up her heart and her mind, and for not being judgmental and holding her accountable for what she didn't know.

My experience shows that you can and should always live your truth, no matter what anyone has to say about you. God made you who you are – a special person, with gifts. You are born for a reason because the world needs you for exactly who you are. If someone tries to make you feel uncomfortable about being who you are, simply educate them on the importance of unconditional love. My wish for you is that, then, you will find the same love and support that came to me.

Love,
Jenee

Public figure Jenee Reed is a professional disc jockey, photographer, and videographer. She is also executive sales manager and CEO for NBT NothingButTalentLLC. She holds a bachelor's degree in secondary education from Shippensburg University. The world traveler and avid reader, born in Philadelphia, now resides in Atlanta, Georgia. "I found a balance being a serial entrepreneur and working in corporate America," she says. "I love being a positive role model in a servant leader.

"He turned around and came out to me."

Dear Friend,

When I look back on what my parents taught me, I remember the good things. Do your best. Treat others as you would have them treat you. Love and respect nature.

I was a "tomboy" and athletic. Call them stereotypes of lesbians, but honestly, I didn't know. I dated a guy in high school and truly loved him but didn't realize that I loved him only as a friend.

In college, I played basketball with a woman who was never around campus on weekends. One day, she said, "You probably wonder where I go every weekend. I'm going to visit a girlfriend."

And then it hit me. "Oh, boy. I am gay." That woman and I started dating. I was 19 years old.

I waited until my mid-20s to come out to my younger brother. He turned around and came out to me. I had no idea. We decided not to tell our mom right away.

Remember, of course, that my family believed that we are part of a society, and we should all be good citizens. I had no reason to believe that I would run into issues, and I was right. I was 30 when I told my mom – my dad had died when I was a kid – and she was very accepting. She worried that my life would be hard, but her attitude toward me didn't change. "I love you," she said. "It doesn't matter to me."

I never ran into adverse attitudes. I was working in the health insurance industry and had no pushback. In that regard. I was lucky. But it began to dawn on me that representation matters. These were the AIDS years, and we were all so nervous about being "outed," but I decided that people just had to get to know us. If they saw us as neighbors and friends, they would realize that we are not "abnormal."

After all, the change in attitudes about marriage equality had to do with the visibility of LGBTQ people. That doesn't happen when people are closeted. The general representation of LGBTQ people in the media has been positive and helpful, but when it comes down to it, knowing folks on a personal level makes all the difference.

I'm in my 60s, and my story is much gentler than the coming-out stories of many others from my generation. When I compare the no-big-deal attitude of my nieces and nephews to the sheer panic that we felt, I am absolutely floored.

I met my wife and partner of 26 years on a blind date. Really? My gym owner's wife happens to know two lesbian women, and she figures we would just love each other? Well, we met for drinks, and that was that. And the friend who introduced us? She was at our wedding.

I don't have lessons to share from hardship, but a blessed life can reveal a few gems, too. First, find LGBTQ friends. It just helps.

And keep representing. That is crucial. This world has become more expansive, but it needs to stay that way. The same representation that opened doors decades ago now has to keep those doors propped open. After all, LGBTQ equality still isn't written into law. We have to do two things at once – make progress, and don't allow things to slide back to where they were.

Just as I was taught, the key to happiness is staying true to yourself, but also, doing good for others. Stand up with pride for yourself and the LGBTQ community, and the world will be a better place.

With love,
Shawn Scott

Shawn was born, raised, and still resides in the Harrisburg, Pennsylvania area. She went to college in western Pennsylvania and has worked in the health insurance industry for 35 years. She and her wife enjoy travel, standard poodles, and the Jersey Shore. A proud Democrat, Shawn believes most strongly in equality and quality education for all.

"The haters are wrong, not you."

Dear Friend,

Growing up LGBTQ, you will hear bad things. Maybe you'll believe them, like I did. Homosexuality was wrong, I was taught, so how could I be that? Homosexuals led sad lives, they said, and I didn't want to be sad.

Then I saw with my own eyes that none of it was true. I met amazing people leading amazing lives, and they were LGBTQ. I didn't have to believe the doubters. I could believe in myself and the true friends I made.

I grew up in a wonderful way, on a farm in the country. I would walk through the cornfield and over the "crick," to grandmother's house I'd go. My cousins lived down the street. I was involved in fun youth activities at the megachurch my family attended.

And I knew I was gay. It was "wrong," I was taught. So like St. Paul, I prayed that God remove this thorn from my side. Nothing changed. My need to reconcile my Christianity with my sexuality grew stronger. In college, I met a chaplain who also advised the campus LGBTQ group. Suddenly, a pathway opened.

I took my mom to a coffee shop and told her. She worried that my life would be sad, but I tried to keep a positive attitude. The leaders of my church pushed back, even telling the kids I counseled at church camp that they couldn't talk to me. One of the kids cried and told me he still loved me.

When things like that happen, you realize that the haters are wrong, not you. But I still didn't know that I could be happy, until two people changed my life. Both were alumni of my college - a prominent physician, and a filmmaker - who became my professional and personal mentors.

Two moments opened my eyes. At a birthday party, I saw my doctor friend living the "family-man" life with his husband, which is what I've always wanted.

And the filmmaker invited me to a human rights campaign gala. There I was, arriving in my beat-up Pontiac and wearing my only suit

- so tragic – but I was mingling with highly successful businessmen who were also gay.

I saw my friends' lives up close, and – what a wonder! – they were both happy and accomplished. You realize the world is small and interesting. You just have to live in it and say yes to opportunities.

Now, I own an accounting firm. I'm a leader in party politics. My husband and I live in a country town. We are highly involved and feel warmth and acceptance from our neighbors.

I have experienced all the privileges that society gives a white male. I'm so grateful for everything that LGBTQ activists have done for us, but there is much more to do, especially for Black and Brown and transgender people. Fortunately, we're seeing more role models on TV and in politics.

But I also believe that everyone can be a role model, TV star or not. If people see you living your authentic life, they will get to know you for who you are. That is changing the world.

Hope is out there. You can start by being patient. My parents needed time to come to grips with my sexuality, just like I did. Today, we're as close as we've ever been.

Also, find your personal role models, the people who are living the life you want to lead. I was blessed with those role models, and they helped me realize that everything would be okay.

It is okay. Your good life is out there. Find the happiness you deserve.

Your friend,
Alex Reber

Alexander Reber, CPA, MBA, is managing partner of Miller Dixon Drake, PC, a CPA firm in downtown Harrisburg, Pennsylvania. He has served in leadership in many organizations including, currently, elected Treasurer of the PA Democratic Party and the past board chair of Planned Parenthood Keystone. His public service includes serving on the Harrisburg City Audit Committee and as a member of the Legislation Committee of the Pennsylvania Institute of CPAs.

CHAPTER 8

"Everybody's journey is individual. If you fall in love with a boy, you fall in love with a boy. The fact that many Americans consider it a disease says more about them than it does about homosexuality."

- James Baldwin

CHAPTER 8

NOTES

....

....

....

....

....

....

....

....

....

....

....

....

....

....

....

....

....

....

....

....

"It was the elephant in the room."

Dear Friend,

"How could you do this to me?"

It's hard to imagine a harsher reaction to telling a loved one that you're gay, but I really did hear that. To this cousin, her feelings mattered more than mine. Here I am, 33 years old, and I still struggle to be fully open because of reactions like that. Deep down, though, I know that knowing who I am is the only way to be truly happy and healthy.

My story begins with how I was raised. In my Afro-Latino home, there was a "right" way to be, and that was heterosexual. Any other way was a sin. My mother and grandmother were very religious. If you weren't straight, then something was wrong with you mentally. In that world, homosexuality was a perversion.

But you notice things about yourself that don't line up with what you're taught to believe. I only liked the company of girls, but not in a sexual manner. Around guys, I always felt nervous, anxious, and uncomfortable. Was it because I liked them, or was I just nervous? I worried that the guys would judge me or "figure me out" and call me gay. Kids only know what they're taught, and like me, they were taught that being gay was bad.

I've never officially announced that I'm gay. I told a few people when I was in my early 20s. One cousin said she still loved me, no matter what, but others grilled me with questions that seemed to imply I had made some kind of selfish choice. My mother had always suspected and would blow up in anger about it, so I really couldn't discuss it with her. It was the elephant in the room. To my regret, we never really had the frank discussions we should have had, and there are consequences of that failure. I experience depression today, and I believe that at least some of it comes from that lack of truthfulness in my home.

Accepting myself is a work in progress. I'm still dealing with how to fully be me when so many people have rejected that person. Maybe I worry too much that, somehow, I'm hurting the feelings of other people. I want to please them, but I also have to remember that in time, people realize you are just who you are, and they have to accept you for that.

When I told my grandmom I was gay, she said, "That's a lonely life." And in actuality, it can be, because too many people feel you shouldn't be this way. But – and this is the important part – if you aren't true to yourself, your mental health with suffer. You'll be sad because you're not being genuine.

If you need help, seek it out. Talk to somebody who can relate to or understand what you're going through. Open up to someone who can help you accept yourself and live your life without worrying about the judgment of others.

The lesson of my experience, even the unhappy times, is: Be true to who you are. If others don't accept you, then they won't. You will learn how to deal with that. Never let anyone try to dim your light. Keep it shining, and it will guide your way.

Love,
Josh

Joshua Wilson is originally from Philadelphia and currently living in New York City. He studied business and now works for a shipping company. With a talent for sewing and designing, which he has always used as a coping mechanism, he founded his own business, Styles by Joshy, @StylesByJoshy, to create custom apparel. He loves music and listens to a broad array, but his favorite genres are R&B and reggae.

"It does not have to be scary."

Dear Future Queers,

I've always accepted that I was part of the LGBTQ community. To be honest, there was not a real journey. This is something that should be taught more and spoken about. Not everyone has a long-tortured journey of acceptance. Sometimes you have a sort of natural acceptance. You just realize that you are LGBTQ, and that is it.

When I was younger, I was lucky to have a very accepting family. It is a privilege that I am very thankful for. My parents have been surrounded their whole lives by friends who are members of the LGBTQ community and grew up with parents who were also accepting of all kinds of people.

My parents never hid LGBTQ issues or content away from me or my brother. That included my parents' friends who were LGBTQ. They were part of our family, just like anyone else. I was lucky to have had that experience, too.

Obviously, my parents never believed that being gay was a sin or anything in that regard. My parents taught me that people who thought that way were being ignorant and hateful. But having a supportive family still is not enough to hide you from all the controversy and hate that comes from people who do not accept you. Thankfully, I have not had to deal personally with people who did not accept me, but as I grew up and became friends with other LGBTQ people, I heard and saw their experiences, which breaks my heart.

Now you see that my coming out story is not very exciting, simply because I never had to "come out." Honestly, that is the way it should be. My parents never forced me to come out or to label myself. I just knew during middle school that I was not straight. I did not know my label, and I still really do not know it yet to this day, but I knew I was not like everyone else.

Regardless of how I felt deep inside, my parents were very supportive and accepting, not once forcing me to label myself.

Maybe this won't seem like the most inspirational story. But more LGBTQ people should realize that their story does not have to be big or tragic or inspirational. It can just be what it is.

Before I finish, there are a few things that I want the next generation to know:

• Your journey of being LGBTQ is not linear. You might not know your label, and that is okay. Labels are helpful for some people, and for others they are not.

• There are too many stories about tragically coming out. We need to uplift and spotlight the stories of acceptance and found family. Sharing only the stories of tragedy and non-acceptance scares the younger generation. I want them to know that it does not have to be scary.

• Your journey is at your own pace. Your journey can continue up until you are 20s, 30s, or longer. It is not about the destination, but rather the journey.

• Being LGBTQ is not something to be scared about.

If you do not have a story of acceptance like me, I hope you will find your people. Family does not have to be the one that you are biologically related to. That is a big benefit of our community. We get to choose our family.

Best of luck in your future,
Sydney George

Sydney George is a graduate of Carlisle High School and a student at Millersville University, both in Pennsylvania. She is studying speech communications with a focus in theater. She has been involved with local LGBTQ organizations in high school and college, and she actively participates in local theater productions.

"Everyone is welcome to be just who they are."

Dear Future Queers,

We are writing as parents who believe with all our hearts that family are the people who love you for who you are, whether they are the family you're given or the family you find.

We both grew up in typical middle-class homes, without a whole lot of diversity in our white, Catholic upbringing during the 1970s and '80s. What we both had in common was being raised to respect others and value learning.

As each of us headed to college life, we gravitated to diverse friend groups, with different backgrounds, with various interests, who taught us more about arts and culture and the world. What the college experience taught us was to keep learning - not just in the classroom and not just from books - and to keep an open mind.

Fast forward to the two of us meeting and marrying in 1991, and then having two children. We have both always been committed to surrounding ourselves and our kids with good people - people who support one another and who make good choices. When they do not make good choices, they learn from their mistakes. None of that has anything to do with one's gender or sexuality.

So, when our teenage daughter shared with us that she's not straight, but queer, what were we to say? What does that truly matter? It's her life and who she chooses to share it with is her decision.

We have raised her to be responsible, curious, kind, loving and strong. That was our job, and how she lives her personal life is up to her. Our only hope is that she finds a partner who values her and loves her as much as we do. That's it, that's all the criteria we have -- an emotionally healthy, respectful relationship. That is all any parent should want for their child, straight or gay.

As a couple married almost 30 years, we hope we have provided an example for a committed, solid relationship. So have many of our gay friends who, likewise, have been in committed relationships and/or married for just as many years. Our job as parents is to either be role models or make sure your children are surrounded by people who can be role models for your children.

We have also, hopefully, made our home a safe and welcoming space for not only our children but their friends. Everyone is welcome to be just who they are when they are with us. We will help and support anyone along their journey. It's just the right thing to do.

Please know that we are not unique in that regard. There are people out there - couples, parents, grandparents - who can also provide, and want to provide, your safe and welcoming space.

We have often heard that gay people get to choose their own family. So, be sure to choose the right people to be around. No one should make you feel unworthy, or lesser, or a disappointment.

You absolutely deserve unconditional love and support. If you do not have it, we hope you find it, or it finds you. Just know that there are people out there who WILL accept you. Find them. Look for us. We are here for you.

Barrie Ann & Joseph George

Barrie Ann George was born in Easton, Pennsylvania, and earned degrees at Shippensburg University. She is the vice president of a non-profit organization. Joseph George was born in Morristown, New Jersey, and graduated from Dickinson College. He is in sales and owns a DJ business. Meeting in Harrisburg, Pennsylvania, they settled in Carlisle, Pennsylvania, where they raised their two children. In addition to their careers, they also write a fine arts column for two local newspapers.

"I stood in front of a mirror crying."

Dear Friend,

I'm lucky that my story is one of acceptance, and maybe that's why I find satisfaction in advocating for others who are LGBTQ. You never know how the good things you do will inspire others, and that makes life a great place to be.

I grew up in a religious family that never judged others. My uncle was gay, and he was accepted, but it was a double-edged sword. I was confident that my family would give me the same acceptance, but sadly, my uncle was not a good role model. He had a lot of issues in his life, and in my mind, those problems were all wrapped up in his being gay.

I was 13 years old when I stood in front of a mirror crying, saying, "I can't be like my uncle. I can't be like my uncle." Fortunately, time heals. When I was 17, I realized that I didn't have to be like him, that my life could be happy and fulfilling.

Coming out was – well, a bit traumatic. My sister blurted out the news to my parents, and there was a big fight just as I was leaving for work. When I came home, things were calmer, and my parents made it clear that they simply hadn't wanted this for me, but they understood that it wasn't a choice.

Plus, a girl I was "dating" told everyone at school. Yes, I got called names, but I didn't lose any friends. I was the first person to come out at my school, and the funny thing is that the people I knew were gay kind of avoided me, like they were scared of being associated with me.

So, I didn't "come out" in the traditional sense. I was "brought out." But I never denied it. My attitude toward others: If you don't like it, you don't like it.

Then something amazing happened. During my first year in college, one of my high school teachers told me that I had started a positive movement there. Other kids were coming out because they felt safe. This teacher was providing some guidance to them, and she asked if I would talk to anyone who wanted to contact me.

Of course! No one ever called, but I could look back and realize that by being myself and proud and calm, I started a wave that freed so many people from their fear.

Now, I'm happy to talk to anyone who's worried or struggling with being LGBTQ. My message comes from my deep religious beliefs. Trust in who you are. You have to be yourself. God made you for a reason, and your story needs to be told. You will have support and love if you just have faith.

If your family struggles to accept you, counseling can be a big help. There is always an answer. You have a full life ahead of you. You can educate others and make your life a positive thing. There is an angel out there for you.

Here's a story about my college years. Some of us created an improv group that performed skits in the dorms and ended up touring other schools. We won awards, but more importantly, we tackled tough issues like AIDS and drug abuse. So many students came up to us after our shows and said, "You saved my life. You made me realize that it's okay and I'm not alone."

How powerful is that?! If you can find that kind of belonging and purpose, you'll realize that life is great. You can help others. You can be that angel.

With love and support,
Brian Miller

Brian Miller, MKBD, is an award-winning, certified kitchen and bathroom designer from Harrisburg, Pennsylvania. He holds a bachelor's degree in interior design and Spanish from Indiana University of Pennsylvania, and an MBA in business from Millersville University. He volunteers for animal rescues and fosters animals in need of love and support. His friends and family are everything, and he lives life to the fullest, spending quality time with loved ones to create new adventures together.

QUOTES

"No pride for some of us without liberation for all of us."

– Marsha P. Johnson

CHAPTER 9

NOTES

....
....
....
....
....
....
....
....
....
....
....
....
....
....
....
....
....
....
....
....

"Everyone has value, especially you."

Dear Friend,

Brian and I went to school together since kindergarten. It was an era when we were taught that girls wore pink and played with dolls, and boys played sports and got dirty. Brian didn't. He preferred chorus over PE and wore colorful clothes to school and chose the rainbow lunchbox.

Brian was like a magnet that attracted our attention... everyone's attention, boys and girls. He loved every minute of it. You might think he was bullied for being different, for standing out so much. But he wasn't. He had this inner confidence and always seemed happy. I guess we didn't know a word for being gay back then. All the girls had a crush on him, and he liked us well enough, but not in the way we wanted. He came out in high school, and it all made sense.

I'm still friends with Brian, and he's as colorful as ever! One of his recent social media posts read "believe so deeply until it manifests for you." Wow. This resonated as so very "Brian!" He believed in happiness. He believed in love. He believed in himself all along. There is no other way that a kid could have manifested so much confidence at such a young age. He just loved himself for who he was and continues to be true to who he is today.

Everyone wants to be loved. Everyone. It's just part of being human. And love is bigger than just romantic love. Did you know that the ancient Greeks defined more than four kinds of love? They are also referenced in the Bible. Eros is romantic love. Philia is brotherly love. Storge is family love. And Agape is divine love. Agape love is defined as unselfish love between God and humans and humans' love for mankind.

Love is a feeling of connection with another person. Love is not only good for our spirit, it's good for our health and wellness.

Before any form of love can be experienced, a person must love themselves. The Greeks had a word for this, too. Self love is called Philautia. In a healthy sense, Philautia means taking care of yourself. It's liking yourself, and you've got to like yourself before you can love anyone else... no matter who!

So, how do you go about liking yourself? First, be kind to yourself. Think positive thoughts about yourself. Even if you don't feel like you fit in or if you don't feel like you're deserving of love, YOU ARE. Everyone has value, especially you. Second, every day write something good about yourself in a journal or in some kind of notes. Do you like that you're tall or that you're good in math? Do you like your voice or like your sense of humor? Write something down every single day.

Once you start to "feel the love," you'll be ready to share it. Sharing love is simply kindness. The more kindness you share, the more it comes back to you, and love will grow and grow in your life. So how do you go about sharing kindness? Start with just smiling at someone. Your smile will cause them to smile back! Just think of Brian who smiled at everyone and who still does today!

With kindness, love, and positivity, you'll find your tribe. All those good things you're writing about yourself will be seen, appreciated, and loved by your true friends.

One of my favorite quotes says that when you are kind to others, it not only changes you, it changes the world.

Being kind is always worth the effort! Good luck!

With love,
Una Martone

As president and CEO of Leadership Harrisburg Area, Una has grown the organization and its community impact. She also serves at the local, regional, and international levels of Rotary International, training international leaders and supporting clean water initiatives, emergency relief, international peace fellowships, and polio eradication. Una, the youngest of seven siblings, is a first-generation American whose parents were born in Ireland. She and husband of 28 years, Mike, have two children, Michael and McCaffrey.

"I end up marrying the guy!"

Dear Friend,

My mom used to say that I was an "old soul." It was a nod to my sensitivity and calmness. Nobody talked much about gay life, but when kids would call each other names like "sissy," it stung me a bit. I had a feeling they were talking about people like me, because I had more crushes on boys than I did on girls. To my mind, boys were just more crush-worthy.

Coming out was very difficult, and when I was a teenager, I started drinking and using substances. Genetics were a factor, but I also felt like I had no clear path forward with reconciling my sexuality.

Finally, I became tired of the disorder in my life. I was drawn toward normalizing life and being true to who I was. With help from a really good therapist, I became sober at 32.

Around this time, I made my first really good gay friends. I was working in health care, where the LGBTQ community was, and is, well represented. They showed me that I could have a healthy, open life that wasn't about gay bars. I could be honest with myself and with everybody else.

I came out to the people I was closest to, starting with my sister. Nobody was surprised, and they were wonderful. It was really a nonevent. My boss actually thanked me for trusting her with this news.

My next goal was finding a meaningful relationship, but that's hard to do when you're moving around and building a career. Fast forward to my early 40s, and I relapsed in my sobriety. The relapse lasted four years, until I got treatment and emerged with a clearer sense of the self-acceptance that remained to be done.

A couple of years later, I went on a date with a guy and we clicked. Still, I said I wasn't looking for a relationship. That's okay, he said.

Here we are, 16 years later, a happily married couple. All those years I wanted a relationship, and nothing came along. Then I tell someone I don't want a boyfriend, and I end up marrying the guy!

Which is a great way of saying that the journey never ends. Today, I am determined, after my protracted coming-out process, that I will always be clear about who I am. I'm gay and sober, and these are foundational to who I am.

Honestly, LGBTQ people are some of the toughest people I know. You've got to have steel inside. You have to have a tough core to insert yourself day after day into situations where you may be the only LGBTQ person in the room.

I'd like to offer advice about career and life. Don't worry what your LGBTQ status will do to your career. Just be smart and work hard. That's the thing people care about, and it's always the key to success.

As for life, I speak as someone who's been in recovery for 20 years. While substance use isn't limited to the LGBTQ community, it certainly is an issue for many of us. Be sure to care for yourself. If your partying is becoming unhealthy, talk to someone sooner rather than later. Life gets a million times better when you pay attention and get in recovery.

Finally, if you're not out, don't let others determine your schedule. Do it at your own pace and comfort level. If you are struggling to come out, find some good gay friends. Find people you want to be like. It offered me a view of what's possible, and it can do the same for you.

Your friend,
Gil Brown

Gil Brown has been Chief Executive Officer of Hospice of Central Pennsylvania since 2013. He brought to the organization over 30 years' experience in healthcare operations and leadership with Hospice by the Sea, in Florida; New York City Health and Hospital Corporation; Continuum Health Partners; and Aetna Health Plans.

Gil has a B.A. in psychology from Bloomsburg University and an M.S. in Organizational Behavior from the University of Hartford's Barney School of Business.

"I can be any gender I feel like I am!"

Dear Friend,

The first thing to tell you is that I am 8 years old, and I am genderfluid. Even though I am young, I have been taught to be yourself and to believe what you want to believe. I was taught to make good decisions and to help other people make good decisions. I have learned to share emotions with other people so they can learn to be themselves.

My mom said I started exploring gender when I was 3 or 4 years old. When I was 8, I started thinking about it more. My parents tell me to be myself, and that made me think, "You know what? I can be any gender I feel like I am!"

So, when I'm eating lunch at school, I feel like a boy because I want to show people, they can be themselves and eat however they want to. Then at recess, I feel agender because I like to play with everyone and just be myself. At the end of the day, when my mom or dad picks me up from school, I feel genderfluid, because you shouldn't have to be afraid to be whatever you want to be.

When I turned 8 and started thinking about this, I began to talk with my sister, Raina. She talks about different genders and things like "bisexual" and "pansexual." That helped me feel like I could accept myself. I need her in my life because I can talk to her and she helps me get through things.

When I wanted to tell my friends that I was nongender, my mom helped me tell my teacher. Then my teacher helped me tell my friends. I chose a different name that I wanted to be called: Uoago. One of my friends was fine with calling me Uoago, but he liked my birth name, Jules, better, so he calls me by both names.

If you are scared to tell people about your gender or sexuality, my advice is: Don't worry about what other people think. Just be yourself. Try to tell your parents slowly, and maybe they'll accept you. If they don't and you have a best friend, you can tell that friend, and hopefully, they will understand.

Then, slowly, you can tell everyone and – Boom! Hopefully, they'll be okay with it! To people who don't think it's okay, I would say, "Why can't you just support people? One day, you might feel different, and people might judge you, but I don't want them to judge you."

Remember, we should all be able to be ourselves. Have fun, and just explore!

Love,
Uoago

P.S. This is Raina speaking! The best thing you can do to help someone is just to be there for them. Don't be afraid to ask questions or make suggestions. And listen to them. If they aren't sure what gender they are, they don't have to make a decision, but if they want to make that decision, it's best to talk through it to figure it out.

The genderfluid Uoago (Jules) is in second grade. They like collecting Pokemon and have fun battling with friends. Uoago's favorite subject is art, especially sketching and painting. Uoago also likes bunnies – "They're very aggressive, but cute," they say – and has a bunny named Roaxy. Uoago's sister is always there for them. Their favorite color is dark peach. When Uoago is an adult, they might want to be an artist or a veterinarian.

"And of course, my father was looking."

Dear Friend,

As a kid, I had the best of both worlds. I loved sports, like baseball and running. I also liked occasionally playing with the girls in my neighborhood. Sometimes, we played a game that involved shaking your hips to a silly song, pretending to be a senorita. Well, one day, I was going upstairs and absentmindedly did that little "senorita shake," and of course, my father was looking. Needless to say, I got an earful! "It comes from playing with those girls," he said.

My dad grew up in a tough time, and he did not tolerate "weakness" in any way, shape, or form. There I was, though, as expressive then as I am now. I didn't identify as gay, even though I'd have crushes on boys. But as they say, hindsight is 20/20. How could anybody not know I was gay?

I can't say that I heard anything disparaging about being gay, but I heard the remarks. People would be snide about a drag queen who lived in our neighborhood, and I knew in my heart that I would hear those kinds of things if I came out. So I decided to avoid romance altogether.

College finally snapped me out of it, and even then, it wasn't until my junior year. I was finally meeting other gay people. It was the spring of 1984, and so many people around me – good friends of mine – were coming out that I wondered, "Is there something in the water?"

I was mesmerized. It seemed totally inconceivable that I could be one of them, and yet, the dynamics were changing. Here were friends who were comfortable coming out to me, and it was a revelation. The biggest struggle for me had been the idea that I had to stay silent about myself. Finally, that was no longer the case. I had people I could confide in. They showed trust in me, so I could trust them. That made it so much easier for me to accept myself!

There was still the matter of my family, though. After college, I moved from my hometown of Philadelphia to Harrisburg, so it was easy to keep that part of my life a secret. When I showed up at a family wedding with passion marks on my neck, my brothers – I'm one of five boys in a family of six! – teased me and asked, "What's her name?"

I made up a girl's name and changed the subject.

The thing to know about me is that I still haven't officially "come out" to my family, but like I said, how could they not know? I have a boyfriend I love, and I have taken him home to meet my mother. I have a circle of friends I love and trust. Friends have tried to push me to come out to family members, but I know my family, and I know myself. I don't deal well with conflict, and someone could say something that could force me to defend myself and disrupt the relationships I've built all my life.

I can't say that's the best way of doing it, but there is no right or wrong way. I would never advise anyone else to come out against their will, and I wouldn't advise them to hold back, either. This is your journey, and you choose the paths to follow. No matter where those roads take you, remember that you don't have to keep your feelings bottled up. Find the people you can trust and confide in, and it does make it easier.

Love,
David

David Payne was born and raised in Philadelphia, the youngest of six. He earned a bachelor's degree in communications from Temple University. With his passion for news and broadcasting, he is a reporter and anchor for the Radio Pennsylvania Network in Harrisburg, PA. Since 2002, David has served as the voice of the Temple University Diamond Marching Band. David enjoys theater (both attending and performing), and he never met a karaoke bar he didn't like.

"You will surely evolve and refine."

Beloveds,

Woven into Pride Month messages of belonging are renewed calls for advocacy. In Pennsylvania, the governor has again called for elected officials to pass comprehensive non-discrimination protections for LGBTQ Pennsylvanians. President Biden has asked Congress to pass the Equality Act, making these protections effective for all Americans. The president even signed the first Juneteenth National Independence Day Act, establishing a holiday to commemorate the end of slavery and reminding everyone that all of our liberations are connected.

I grew up in Central Pennsylvania, the adopted son of a Protestant minister. My mother and father loved me in the ways they could, but I often suspected that the pressures to maintain the image of a minister and his family often prevented us from authentically connecting as individuals and as a family.

As I entered junior high school, I began to internally recognize that I was, in some ways, different from my peers. I didn't have an openly queer member of my family, I didn't go to school with anyone who was "out," and the only LGBTQ-related references I encountered came from the church, along with negative reactions and consequences. To combat loneliness, food became my source of personal comfort. It also let me use my weight as the excuse for not dating girls.

Once in college, it all began to change. I was forced to grow, to become uncomfortable, and to fully comprehend the existence of a more diverse and global world than the homogenous and fragile bubble I occupied. I learned much about others and, perhaps more importantly, about myself. I started living authentically in my identities just after my college graduation, but in a slow and calculated process with hundreds of "coming out" moments.

For friends, they were moments of joy and celebration. For most colleagues, they were moments of reflection and inspiration. And for my parents, almost a decade after starting this process, they were moments of struggle and growth.

Living authentically increased my confidence and self-esteem, which allowed me to achieve and maintain a healthy lifestyle. Professionally,

I have had the privilege of supporting queer and questioning students for two decades. I've marched in Pride parades. I've worked with organizations fighting for an equitable world for all, and I was even appointed as the nation's first Executive Director for a statewide commission on LGBTQ Affairs in Pennsylvania.

You may find that aspects of my story resonate with you or that your own journey has taken a different path. Regardless, a few things will likely remain true. There will be moments of challenge that show you the breadth of determination and resilience within you, and there will be moments of joy and achievement that surpass any of your wildest dreams.

Let me also remind you of a few facts. You are worthy and you are enough. You will surely evolve and refine, but your worth will never be in question. Remember to be strong, to be powerful, to be beautiful, and to interpret all of those in the ways that are most meaningful to you.

Finally, do not forget that you are admired and loved. And when you read this, I will be here. I will answer all of your questions on what it was like living through the height of the AIDS crises, through marriage equality, and through the global pandemic of COVID-19. Most importantly, I will be here to learn from you, as you teach me about the new and contemporary issues facing our communities and the ways in which Pride Month demands justice for all.

With deepest admiration,
Todd

Todd Snovel (he, him, his) is Special Assistant to the President and Director of Strategic Initiatives at the Pennsylvania College of Art and Design in Lancaster, Pennsylvania. Before this, he was appointed by Pennsylvania Governor Tom Wolf as the inaugural Executive Director for the Pennsylvania Commission on LGBTQ Affairs.

Todd lives out his passions by contributing to his community and advocating for equality and access to education, the arts, and health care.

CHAPTER 10

"It takes no compromise to give people their rights ... it takes no money to respect the individual. It takes no political deal to give people freedom. It takes no survey to remove repression."

– Harvey Milk

CHAPTER 10

NOTES

....
....
....
....
....
....
....
....
....
....
....
....
....
....
....
....
....
....
....
....

"My heart beat a bit differently when a woman walked by."

Dear Searcher,

Growing up I was always taught, "if you start something, you have to finish it." Despite the occasional boredom or unwillingness, I always finished my group projects, sports season, or commitment made. I was taught to be kind, saying "please" and "thank you" to each elder who deserved my respect.

I was encouraged to always do my best, although I was often my biggest critic. Demanding much from myself at a young age, I achieved academic and athletic accolades with ease. On paper and to most I encountered, I was pretty impressive.

Yet…I never felt impressed, or even good enough to myself.

I always felt a little like my head was in the clouds or that people just didn't understand me. It wasn't until my sophomore year of college that I realized my friends and family would never relate to me, because my heart beat a bit differently when a woman walked by instead of a man.

College opened my eyes to new possibilities, cultures, and experiences. In my junior year, it came to me. No matter how many good grades I got, soccer games I won, or family functions I attended - I would never feel worthy until I learned to speak my truth and love myself.

I first came out to my closest friends and was met with nothing but support and a few general questions. My parents, however, took the conversation a different route. Confusion, anger, and tears spilled out from each of us. My unconditionally loving mother did not want me to have a harder life and worried over how she would protect me. They asked questions. "Are you sure it's not a phase?" "Are you sure you're not being influenced by your gay friends?" "Are you sure you don't need to try more with boys?"

Are you sure, are you sure, are you sure?

After that conversation, I was about as sure as an elephant is stable on stilts.

Things were certainly awkward and emotional over the next few years. My family may have been confused and concerned at first, but their love never faded. They made sure to tell me that at the end of each hard conversation. I am very lucky compared to most, and now finally, five years later, my family and I can openly talk and even joke about being gay.

I didn't want to disappoint my family or be the black sheep.

I didn't want my life to be judged or harder than necessary.

I didn't want my choices to be associated with stereotypes or unconscious biases.

What I did know, however, was that I wanted to be authentic.

My body ached and my mind wandered to dark places with each day spent in hiding.

I finally told myself no more hiding, as I was sure that being gay was my truth.

Just like I am sure this is my story. I started it and now I cannot wait to finish it.

To my fellow LGBTQ friends, I hope you grow the confidence and self-love to accept yourself. Things take time, so you should not feel pressured to come out to everyone all at once, or even officially come out at all. Take things day by day and know that even on your darkest days, if you just breathe and rest – you will get through. You have friends to make, adventures to take, foods to try, art to create, movies to see, and so much more. Your sexuality should not shame you into missing out on anything life has to offer. Now go be confident, and write your own story.

Yours on the journey,
Kristin Dobransky

Kristin Dobransky is a Penn State and Clemson University graduate now working in health care administration. She enjoys helping others whenever she can or at the very least, making them smile and laugh. In her free time, she enjoys visiting with family and friends, watching football, traveling, and baking.

"I came to the realization that I am who I am."

Dear Friend,

Growing up, my entire life felt different from everyone else's. Not only was I usually the only military kid in my class, but I was also the tallest and the most dramatic and flamboyant. My parents – my father in the Army, and both of them Roman Catholic and headstrong feminists – tried to do their best with me, even though I was the kid that many people considered to be quite a handful.

I was the middle child. I never got along with my brother, the rough-and-tumble boy who was three years younger than me. But I grew close with my sister, six and half years older, because we bonded over music and dance.

In those days, I never even heard the words "gay," "lesbian," or "homosexual." I only knew that I was different, but without any words to put to it, I did not know how.

I was brought up with love and with a belief in the Roman Catholic church. I was taught that God was a loving God. The funny thing is, I didn't hear anyone say that being gay is "wrong" until much later in life.

Whenever I felt alone or out of place, I was fortunate to have people in my world who helped me feel okay with just being me. Some were teachers. Some were shop owners, like the owner of the music store in my hometown. He would greet me with a smile and would talk to me for an hour, offering suggestions of what I might like while I looked through the CDs. He always made me feel safe and able to be who I wanted to be.

It was in high school when I began to realize that being different was going to be a challenge because I wasn't part of the "norm." I was made fun of and pushed around, but I found my escape in music, musical theater, band, and choir.

Things hit bottom at the end of my senior year. After years of hiding my thoughts, trying to come out didn't work out as I'd hoped. I came out to a friend who, unfortunately, did not take the news well and began to tell others. My parents, who loved me no matter what, took the news in a way that was totally unexpected. They knew, they said, that I was a very loving person and loved everyone, but maybe I wasn't really gay. Maybe this was a calling from God to become a priest.

I was shattered. I told them that their reaction made me more confused than ever. I decided to go back in the closet, which is not a healthy place to be because it only means you're suppressing your true self.

My journey to acceptance took years, but I found it by reaching out to the LGBTQ+ community itself. With help from the LGBT alliance at my college, I came to the realization that I am who I am, and I am made just the way I was meant to be. I was 20 years old, and that realization marked the beginning a new phase in my life.

I have learned that every day is a journey to self-acceptance, just like it is for everyone. I still find myself renewing my self-acceptance every day, affirming that I truly am the genuine, loving person I am meant to be. I'm not perfect. No one is, which makes life so interesting because we can all try, every day, to be the best versions of ourselves. My mantra is to find the perfection in imperfection, and others will see the wonderful person who's inside you.

Love,
David

David Kern grew up most of his life in Carlisle, Pennsylvania, after moving around with his military family. He lives with his spouse, Joe, and their nephew, Will, in Harrisburg, PA. The retail operations manager for Midtown Scholar Bookstore in Harrisburg created Drag Story Time there. He is studying Human Services for Drug and Alcohol Addiction Therapy at Penn State. David has been performing in drag for 20 years as his stage persona, Anita Dickson.

"It was the moment when I first chose ME."

Dear Future Queers,

I'd like to share my journey with you. There are moments that are harrowing, when others tried drastic things to make me into something that I was not. The best decision I ever made was to say no to them, and that's the story I want to tell.

I was born in Zimbabwe into a religious home. My church was the foundation of everything to me. Religion dictated who I would associate with, when I would date, when and even where I would get married. I was raised to believe things like: no dating until you are 16, no sex before marriage, and above all else – homosexuality is a sin.

Even though my life was planned out for me, I felt different. But, I believed I was different only because my family was so religious.

When I was a teenager, my family moved to Canada. I made friends, played soccer, and loved school, but I still felt completely different. This time, I chalked it up to being an immigrant.

At 21, I met and got engaged to a man. It was what I was supposed to do, yet I was so unhappy that I finally broke it off and told my mom I would stay single forever. At the same time, my best friend was moving out of the city, and as we said good-bye, she kissed me. My whole world changed in that instant. I had a rush of butterflies and I LOVED being kissed, but I had been taught it was a sin. It meant I was evil, and I risked being kicked out of church and losing my family if I were gay. I decided I was NOT gay.

I went to my church leaders and confessed what I believed were "my sins." We worked out a plan, and I did everything I was asked. I prayed harder, grew my hair long, and wore makeup and dresses. I even agreed to have an "exorcism" and to start conversion therapy.

The entire time, I was becoming aware of my attraction to women. I made friends with women who were also fighting against being gay and sometimes we were intimate, but we always returned to church to repent.

After three years of counseling, they told me I was scheduled to begin electric shock therapy. I left the meeting and sat in my car and cried. No part of me believed that God would want me to shock myself into changing who I was. I decided then and there to never go back. That decision meant I would be excommunicated from my church. It was the moment when I first chose ME and accepted that I was gay. I began the journey of coming out.

My life did not turn out how I expected when I was a kid – but my ONLY regret is that I did not fully accept myself sooner. Instead of living someone else's dream for me, I have created my own. I created a life that I love.

I never felt so free as the day I accepted who I was. I have loved and been loved. I have my own kids and a community of friends and family that support me. It can still be a difficult road, but it is worth it to live your truth. There is love, and light, and support, and a whole lot of acceptance out there.

Best of luck on your journey as you carve out a space for yourself. It is worth it!

Julie

Julie Byrne is a single, lesbian mother of teenage sons. She lives in Northern Alberta, Canada.

"I would never promise you that things will be easy."

Dear Friend,

What is sexuality? What is gender? People think they just know organically what they are, but my story shows you that knowing yourself requires really knowing what sexuality and gender mean. I am asexual, aromantic, and agender, and trust me, that's not easy for people to understand. The important thing is that I've learned to understand what it means to me.

Growing up, no one in my family talked much about sexuality or gender. I knew what everyone else knows, or thinks they know, about people being straight, and male and female.

When I was in sixth grade, a friend came out as bi. Honestly, I didn't think much about it. They like girls and boys, and there was nothing particularly remarkable about it. Then, I started to realize that it wasn't considered "normal," but that made no difference to me, because my friend was still my friend.

The funny thing is, I never thought of myself as being different, either, until one random YouTube video changed my perspective. Why were other people so interested in relationships? I just didn't know. Then I watched that video – I was in seventh grade – and I learned for the first time about lesser-known sexualities. Suddenly I realized – I was part of the LGBTQIA+ community. This was who I am!

I wanted to learn so much more, so I watched a lot more videos about asexuality and being aromantic. I realized it all applied to me. I had never once been interested in someone in a remotely romantic and sexual way. I told my friends about it and, while they were supportive, I'm not sure if they completely understood. While exploring asexuality, I also found out about being agender. I knew that this applied to me as well, but I took my time about what to do next. I chose not to identify as agender and just let the idea float around in my head.

Finally, it happened. I knew inside myself who I was. I came out as agender, aromantic, and asexual to my mom one month ago. Quite obviously, she didn't understand the idea of being asexual, aromantic, or agender, and she chose not to call me by my chosen name and pronouns.

Is this disappointing? Honestly, I'm managing. I still have issues trying to present the way I wish to and getting others to understand what this all means, but the fundamental thing is that I am proud of who I am. There's an amazing comfort that comes from understanding myself and realizing who I am.

I would never promise you that things will be easy. There are a lot of difficulties ahead. But no matter what, you are you. The people who don't understand you or don't support you won't last forever. You can distance yourself from them, or they will eventually understand.

If COVID has taught you anything, it will be that time is a construct – something made up by humans to mark the days and the seasons. You can't put a clock on when people will understand, so you can't predict when and how things will end. Tomorrow will be different, and the day after tomorrow will be different than the day before. Stay true to yourself even when everything else is changing, and in time, the people who matter will realize that they love you for who you are.

Love,
Rei

Rei chose not to share a photo

Rei is 14 years old and a freshman in high school. Their hobbies are mostly drawing and reading. They are asexual, aromantic, and agender.

"I will have your back and help you to carry the load."

Dear Beloved LGBTQ+ Family Members,

I am a proud ally, advocate and accomplice of the LGBTQ community. You are my people, and I am yours.

I see you. I respect you. I admire you. I got you. I support you. Your whole being. Unconditionally. I am very vocal about matters that are important to you. If they are important to you, then they are important to me.

Know your worth and stay close to those who love you unconditionally. Also, please do not assume that your family and friends will reject you if you reveal that you are LGBTQ. Chances are that they already know. You deserve real love, and you deserve to live your life authentically. Do it - unapologetically.

In light of how many bigoted people there are in the world, I know how difficult your journey may be - especially if you are Black. However, I will have your back and help you to carry the load when it is too heavy for you to do so. And many others will too.

You will need to master the art of "clapping back" so that you can handle the bigots who come for you. When they do, please put them in their place. If you do not, they will continue to terrorize you. This will be exhausting. However, we must fight back - for you and those LGBTQ community members who may not have your privilege or courage. However, please try not to put yourself in harm's way. During these moments of advocacy and justice, please ask and expect your allies, advocates and accomplices to stand with you and, in some cases, stand in front of you.

I honor you and those I love the most:
- My niece and her wife: They are a beautiful couple. I love witnessing their love up close and via social media. The social media comments from their family and friends demonstrate they are loved unconditionally from those who love them the most.
- My bisexual niece: She speaks confidently about her sexuality, and she does not care what others think. I love that. I pray she continues to disregard outdated and harmful societal norms.
- My gay boss, mentor and confidante and his husband: I love

122

these men dearly. These are two of the best men I have ever met in my life. Partners for decades, they married after they were legally allowed to do so in Pennsylvania. I was front and center for the ceremony – a day I will never forget.

• My gay cousin: We have socially conservative family members. I am not one of them. Therefore, I told my cousin that they are always welcome to bring their partner to my home. I love my cousin unconditionally and want them to experience love – without the critical gaze of ignorant family members.

• My queer, questioning and transgender friends: No one loves harder than these friends. If we could bottle this love, the world would be a better place. Period.

When you have been surrounded by phenomenal, real and authentic LGBTQ+ family members for years, there is no other choice but to be a proud ally, advocate and accomplice. Actually, this was not a choice for me. It was an honor and a no-brainer.

One last thing… If you haven't already, please be sure to watch all of the seasons of "Pose," a TV series that ran from 2018 until 2021. The TV series evoked a wide range of emotions when I watched it. I hope you will feel a great sense of pride and community if you have an opportunity to watch it. #BestShowEver #YouWillLoveIt #ILovePrayTellAndBlanca

May you live a long, productive, joyful and love-filled life.

Loyally and Unconditionally YOURS,
Dr. Linnie S. Carter

Dr. Linnie S. Carter, APR is the vice president of college advancement at HACC, Central Pennsylvania's Community College, and executive director of the HACC Foundation.

Dr. Carter is also the president and CEO of Linnie Carter & Associates LLC and a founder of Leadership Restores.

Dr. Carter has been happily married to her husband for more than 25 years and is a proud bonus mom and grandmom, daughter, sister, aunt, godmother and mentor.

"Equality means more than passing laws. The struggle is really won in the hearts and minds of the community, where it really counts."

– Barbara Gittings

NOTES

AFTERWORD

"For a young LBGTQ person, the future is now."

Dear Friend,

My path from a Mississippi Delta childhood to publishing this book is full of twists and turns, and sometimes I took the road not taken. I cherish the people I've met and the friendships I've made along the way. Kind people, gentle people, funny people - and many are LGBTQ+, teaching me that every person we meet helps us to grow.

As a child, I was taught that being "gay" was a sin. And yet, I didn't quite buy it. I knew good people who seemed to be gay, and I accepted them as friends. This doesn't mean that old preconceptions just fled my brain. No. I had to make a conscious decision to question that which I was taught. I was guided by an inner voice reminding me that those teachings were somehow not right.

My LGBTQ friends have taken me by the hand and have taught me so much, though I have so much to learn.

I am inspired by your quiet strength.
I am energized by your bold advocacy.
I am motivated by your persistence.
I am enlightened by your ingenuity.
I am awakened by your wisdom.

Over the years, it has been a privilege to know and work with many talented, passionate people from the LGBTQ community. As I started thinking about how I could help celebrate Pride Month 2021, I remembered a favorite book called "Letters to a Young Brother" by Hill Harper. He offers advice and encouragement to Black young men who rarely see themselves reflected in a positive light. In book clubs, we had fantastic discussions about its messages. The experience had a lasting effect on me.

So, I asked myself, "Why not do something similar for queer people?" They struggle against stereotypes. They endure rejection by loved ones and, amazingly, rise above the challenges and find success.

However, that process takes time, and for a young LGBTQ person, the future is now. Those who can't see hope over the horizon can be drawn toward depression, substance abuse, homelessness and worse.

I ask that you take the adversities of life that you will face and use them to propel yourself forward. Let the negative energy that you encounter be the combustion that drives your engine of success. Let the adversity of life be the ladder that you use to climb higher than anyone could imagine. Let the rejections of life be used to weave a rope to pull you closer to happiness. Then, share your testimony with others. When you share your story of triumph with others, it's like launching a lifeboat to save them from drowning.

This is what Martin Luther King Jr. meant when he said, "In a real sense all life is inter-related. All men are caught in an inescapable network of mutuality, tied in a single garment of destiny. Whatever affects one directly, affects all indirectly."

I support, stand and celebrate with my LGBTQ sisters, brothers and them, joined by an inseparable bond.

This book is filled with inspirational stories from people who find joy and purpose, and some who are still trying to find their way. There is power in their diversity. I hope you find reassurance in these letters. Gift it to those who are struggling to find their way or who lack a support system - or who cling to old prejudices.

My deepest thanks go to the brave people who take us along on their journeys. They made a very personal choice to give back, even dredging up memories of times when society made them feel not valued. They put down the words so they can help you see that life is a journey that leads to love.

With the greatest admiration,
Floyd Stokes

Floyd Stokes, LHD, is the founder and executive director of the American Literacy Corporation (ALC), a non-profit promoting reading to children. He is the author of more than 20 children's books. Floyd's honors include the James Patterson PageTurner Award and the renaming of his high school library in his honor. He has read to children in all 50 states. He lives in Harrisburg, Pennsylvania. Learn more about his work at www.superreader.org.

ACKNOWLEDGEMENTS

This book was made possible by the generous support of Capital Blue Cross.

Special thanks to the many who devoted their time and talents:

• David Skerpon and Rhonda Laing who were instrumental in making this project a reality with their guidance and support.
• Christina Zeigler, the first person I called and asked, "What do you think about us creating a book for the LGTBQ community?" She has been my right-hand person from the start. We have spent hours on the phone and sent countless emails discussing this labor of love.
• Members of the community who helped shape an idea into a concept: Janelle Crossley, Christina Zeigler, Dr. Ski, Sydney George, Tamika Wesley, David Skerpon, and Maxwell Donnelly.
• My intelligent, beautiful and respectful daughters: Madison, for keeping us organized by helping with the behind-the-scenes clerical work, and Olivia, whose thoughtfulness and compassion teach me every day about the importance of caring for others.
• Pauline Medori for allowing us to use her picture of a spreading tree as our cover image.
• Sheena Hisiro for her help with designing the book and the cover. As always, you did a tremendous job!
• George Fernandez for his generous investment in this project and for his willingness to help wherever possible.
• Harvey Freedenberg and Mary Kratzer for their assistance in editing the book.
• Diane McCormick, who interviewed many people to get their stories down on paper. This project wouldn't have happened without you, Diane. You are amazing!

As all of you know, I appreciate you.

Floyd Stokes

This book was created with two purposes in mind.

1. to encourage the next generation of LGBTQ+ youth.
2. to support the educational journey of LGBTQ+ youth.

Proceeds from the sale of this book will fund two scholarships for LGBTQ+ students. A scholarship will be managed and distributed by HACC, Central Pennsylvania's Community College.

The second scholarship will be managed and distributed by the American Literacy Corporation to support LGBTQ+ students who want to attend college anywhere in the United States.

For more information on either scholarship, visit **www.superreader.org/scholarships**.